The Selected
Gwendolyn MacEwen

The Selected
Gwendolyn MacEwen

Edited by
MEAGHAN STRIMAS

Introduction by
ROSEMARY SULLIVAN

Exile Editions

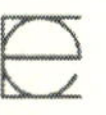

Publishers of
Fiction, Poetry, Essays, Drama, and Art
2007

Library and Archives Canada Cataloguing in Publication

MacEwen, Gwendolyn, 1941-1987.
The selected Gwendolyn MacEwen / edited by Meaghan Strimas ; introduction by Rosemary Sullivan.

(Exile classics ; no. 7)
ISBN 978-1-55096-111-9

I. Strimas, Meaghan, 1977- II. Title. III. Series.

PS8525.E84A6 2007 C818'.54 C2007-906542-2

Cover Photograph by John McCombe Reynolds. Original Artwork by Tony Clark. Design and Composition by MC Design. Typeset in Garamond, Lucida and Cochin. Printed in Canada by Gauvin Imprimerie.

The publisher would like to acknowledge the financial assistance of the Canada Council for the Arts and the Ontario Arts Council, which is an agency of the Government of Ontario.

Conseil des Arts du Canada Canada Council for the Arts

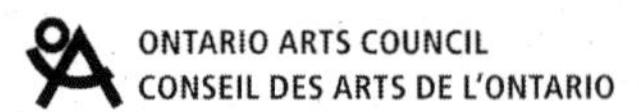

Published in Canada in 2007 by Exile Editions Ltd.
144483 Southgate Road 14
General Delivery
Holstein, Ontario, N0G 2A0
info@exileeditions.com
www.ExileEditions.com

Canadian Sales Distribution:
McArthur & Company
c/o Harper Collins
1995 Markham Road
Toronto, ON M1B 5M8
toll free: 1 800 387 0117

U.S. Sales Distribution:
Independent Publishers Group
814 North Franklin Street
Chicago, IL 60610
www.ipgbook.com
toll free: 1 800 888 4741

Contents

The Drunken Clock ❊ The Rising Fire

• Selections from *The Drunken Clock* (Aleph Press, 1961); *The Rising Fire* (Contact Press, 1963)

Julian the Magician ❊ Terror and Erebus

• Selections from *Julian the Magician* (Macmillan, 1963; Cornith Books in New York, 1963) and *Terror and Erebus: A Verse Play for Radio*, commissioned by CBC Radio One, 1964

A Breakfast for Barbarians

• Selection from *A Breakfast for Barbarians* (1966, The Ryerson Press)

The Shadow-Maker ⁕ The Armies of the Moon

• Selections from *The Shadow-Maker* (Macmillan, 1969); *The Armies of the Moon* (Macmillan, 1972)

King of Egypt, King of Dreams ⁂ Noman ⁂ The Fire Eaters ⁂ Mermaids and Ikons: A Greek Summer

• Selection from *King of Egypt, King of Dreams* (Macmillan in 1971; reissued by Insomniac Press in 2004); Selection from *Noman* (short fiction published in 1972 by Oberon Press);

Afterworlds

The Birds

"Scrapbook"

INTRODUCTION

At the age of ten, Gwendolyn MacEwen wrote her first poem. She saved the pencil with which she wrote it in a sealed white envelope. On the back, in the large lettering of a child, is the date 1951. Precociously, she had determined she would be a poet. At the age of twelve, she insisted that her family was no longer to call her by her nickname Wendy, but rather by her proper name Gwendolyn. As she explained to her sister Carol, she thought one day she might be somebody important, and Wendy was not the name of somebody important. With exquisite determination, she was secretly constructing a myth of her own selection. She became obsessed with magic, attending the shows of the legendary magician Harry Blackstone. "Poets," she would later say, "are magicians without quick wrists." She published her first poem in the prestigious *Canadian Forum* when she had just turned seventeen.

At Toronto's Western Tech High School she wrote stories and poems for the school newspaper *Westward Ho!* in which she railed against those people whose "ability to accept anything that shatters the glass barrier between themselves and the unknown, amounts to nothing." They named her Space Lady in the school yearbook. She took to attending poetry readings at the Y and at the odd café. Looking back in her poem "The Wah Mai Café," she would explain that when the police raided one of the seedier cafés and asked her, the kid in a corduroy jumper, what she was up to, she said she was learning to be a poet: "Actually I'm just a page / But one day I'm going to be a Book."

Gwendolyn MacEwen believed that poetry was a vocation and that there was a language of poetry that required specific training. This was the historical tradition of myths. She was a genuine autodidact with an extraordinary capacity for self-discipline. First, she wanted to study the bible, the Cabala, and the Jewish gnostic mystical tradition. In 1959, just shy of her high-school graduation, she complained that she was not learning the things she needed to know. She left school and made her way to the synagogue, Congregation Knesseth Israel, near High Park, where she asked to be taught Hebrew. If she was to read the bible, she had to do so in the original language. The first book she wrote, at the age of eighteen, but never published, was called *Adam's Alphabet*. With its erudition, allusions, rhythmic rigor, and a certain outrageous prophetic presumption, it is reminiscent of the work of Hart Crane, one of her favourite poets at the time.

The young Gwendolyn MacEwen was driven. The books came, fast and furious. The self-published *Selah* and *The Drunken Clock* in 1961; and *The Rising Fire* with Contact Press in 1963. At that point, she wrote: "My poetry is founded on archaic subjects, or suggestions from such; or – this is more correct – has a thick vein of time flowing through it so that it appears I'm trying to navigate in a fourth dimension. This is true...." She believed that to confine oneself to the contemporary or the personal was to exclude the vast inheritance of myths and stories that have shaped and defined human consciousness. In her novel, *Julian the Magician*, written at age eighteen but not published by Corinth Books until 1963, she creates a strange quasi-medieval world, much like Ingmar Bergman's *Seventh Seal*. Her young magician Julian asks himself a very serious question: When the force of belief reaches a certain point, does a myth become true? Julian is a person seduced by the myths created in his own subconscious.

"A poet doesn't have to be a myopic thing in an attic or a basement," MacEwen wrote. "He or she might well be a dynamic human being, truly involved in the gutsy aspects of life." In 1962, at the age of twenty-one, she travelled alone to Israel, to the heart of the Gnostic tradition that had consumed her youthful reading. But she also needed to understand contemporary politics. She visited Arab villages and saw the tragic inheritance of the Holy Land – Jerusalem, the divided city, was a tacit war zone where enemies looked at each other across a no man's land of hatred and suspicion. An understanding of the brutal politics of power would hereafter inform all her work.

By the time she wrote *A Breakfast for the Barbarians* in 1966, MacEwen had found a larger freedom for her poetic voice. In the loose, incantatory lines of the title poem, she had found a rhythm to carry her meaning: "Eat!" she cried. "The universe fits."

Appetite had become one of her favourite metaphors. It takes a great appetite, what she called "a golden hunger," to live, understanding that what we call the mind is more real than so called material reality. She wanted to consume the world. She felt she was an exile in time and place in the Canada of the early 1960s "so quaint, so naïve, so hopeless."

But, in fact, MacEwen was lucky to be born when she was. In the early 1960s, when she began as a poet, the Canadian cultural community was also coming into its own. At an alternative club in downtown Toronto called the Bohemian Embassy many of the young artists who would go on to shape Canadian literature found comfort in each other's company. MacEwen first met Margaret Atwood at the Bohemian Embassy in 1960. There she also met Jay Macpherson, Margaret Avison, and Phyllis Webb. Al Purdy, Milton Acorn, Dennis Lee, and Joe Rosenblatt were often to be found there, and Leonard Cohen and Irving Layton would drop by when they visiting from Montreal. As Margaret Atwood put it: "You found yourself at the centre very fast in those days. The writing community was so small, beleaguered, and desirous of reinforcement, that it was welcoming to any newcomer with talent, including women." MacEwen and Atwood became close friends, sharing an interest in mythology, discussing Robert Grave's *The White Goddess*, and reading each other's work. Years later Atwood would write the story "Isis in Darkness," a "thinly disguised tribute" to Gwendolyn and those days at the Embassy. To make a living MacEwen was reading manuscripts for Macmillan Publishers and, at the invitation of Robert Weaver, who produced a radio program at the CBC called *Anthology*, she began to write verse plays. She wrote *Terror and Erebus* (1964), a dramatization of the disastrous Franklin expedition in search of the North West Passage and a play called *Tesla* (1966), based on Nikola Tesla, the original inventor of electricity.

In 1964, she turned her attention to Arabic culture, collecting books on Egyptology, and began a serious study of modern Arabic and of hieroglyphics. Soon her notebooks were filled with hieroglyphic drawings as she learned the twenty-four-lettered alphabet, discovering how the language evolved from a combination of ideograms (picture signs) and phonograms (sound signs). Her knowledge became sophisticated enough that she could write her own poems in hieroglyphics. In the spring of 1965, she met and fell in love with a young Egyptian engineer, and was soon speaking Arabic. She shared with him her love of ancient Egyptian culture and of the deserts of his childhood. In 1965 she travelled alone to Egypt to experience first-hand the world of the ancient Pharaohs, for she had determined to write a novel about the eccentric Pharaoh Akhenaton. Akhenaton is credited as the first person in history to have invented the intellectual concept of monotheism. Challenging the hegemony of a politicized priesthood, he imposed his new heretical religion on his reluctant people and created the city of Amarna. Her novel was to be a critique of Akhenaton whose "monotheism was too abstract, too male." Polytheism – a plurality of gods – offered a truer vision of the human psyche. As background to her novel, MacEwen accurately reproduced the geography, military campaigns, political and religious intrigues, cultural customs, including those of childbirth, of ancient Egypt – all the details necessary to bring that world alive. She was being pragmatic and ambitious. She wanted to write a comprehensive and meaty historical novel that might join the ranks of books like Robert Graves' successful *I, Claudius*. The book would become *King of Egypt, King of Dreams* (1971) but while it was published in Canada, it never found an international publisher. Her Arabic had become good enough that she translated a novel by the Egyptian writer Taha Hussein.

At the same time MacEwen was writing one of her finest books of poetry: *Shadow-Maker*, which won the Governor General's Award for Poetry in 1969. In this volume are the famous poems "Dark Pines Under Water" and "Discovery." She had borrowed the concept of chiaroscuro from Leonardo da Vinci: only by seeing the outline of shadow can we recognize the light. The poems are directed inwards, downwards into the dark reaches of the psyche. We run in terror from the dark reaches within ourselves and yet, as she believed, the real mysteries are there. When asked by a rather obtuse interviewer whether she had a mythic imagination, she replied: "Of course. What other kind is there?" "Poets push at reality and come at it from the other side," she said. MacEwen's selected poems *Magic Animals* came out in 1974, and confirmed her growing reputation. Her poems were incantatory. When she gave a poetry reading, believing the essential structure of poetry is musical she recited her poems from memory. Michael Ondaatje remembers how important hearing her read had been to the young writing community. She was the poet people most wanted to hear. When she performed she was mesmerizing.

In 1969 MacEwen met a young Greek musician named Nikos Tsingos. He spoke little English and so she began her study of Greek. Margaret Atwood, who was living outside Toronto, wrote to her friend when she learned of her new lover and asked whether the muse had to come each time bearing a new alphabet. MacEwen and Tsingos were married in Athens in 1971, during which time she wrote her lovely memoir *Mermaids and Icons: A Greek Summer.* Together, through the 1970s, they began to translate works from Greek literature, including *Helen* by Yannis Ritsos, Euripides' *Trojan Women* and Aristophanes' *The Birds*. In 1974 the couple established a coffee house on the Danforth called the Trojan Horse that became a centre for young artists and musicians. It was a *boîte* on the French model, a place where you could talk to friends and, as MacEwen joked, "solve the problems of the universe." Though she and Tsingos had to sell it when it became a financial drain, the Trojan Horse helped to change the shape of Toronto cultural life, eventually becoming a home to Latin-American political exiles fleeing from the dictatorship of Agosto Pinochet.

In 1982 MacEwen produced one of her finest sequences: *The T.E. Lawrence Poems*. Lawrence was for her a complex and lifelong obsession. She had read *The Seven Pillars of Wisdom* as a teenager. In Israel she had encountered an Arab who had ridden with Lawrence. She claimed a family connection – her Aunt Maud and a girlfriend, whose diamond-dealing family met the Lawrence family socially, had visited T.E. (Ned) at Clouds in Dorset, and even stayed overnight in the cottage. Lawrence had been gentle and considerate to the young ladies.

MacEwen even impersonated Lawrence. In a photograph taken by Tsingos on the Island of Antiparos while on their Greek honeymoon, she is wearing a burnous. Tsingos said she jokingly called herself *Lawrence of Antiparos.* She saw T.E. Lawrence as her twin, her male muse, another "Dreamer of the Day," haunting his own deserts. He was, she believed, a failed mystic. In her first-person sequence she writes his narrative from birth to after death, mostly using long lines that hypnotize with their slow rhythm until Lawrence himself seems to surface from the page.

MacEwen's last book *Afterworlds*, published posthumously after her untimely death at the age of forty-six, offers an uncanny sense of looking back and summing up. No doubt this is a delusion simply because we know this was her last book. In "Letters to Josef in Jerusalem" she writes to an Israeli friend from her youth whom she hasn't seen in twenty-five years about the war that has continued uninterrupted for three decades. She returns to scenes of childhood, old lovers. The poems are apocalyptic. In "The Death of the Loch Ness Monster," she takes the perspective of the monster, "tired of pondering the possible existence of man." Have we yet earned the right to call ourselves human? But there are also poems of great affirmation, of tenderness and joy.

Gwendolyn MacEwen was in some strange way an archetype. Her extraordinary talent continues to speak not only in her own works, but also in the works of her contemporaries. Countless poems have been written to her memory and in Timothy Findley's novel *Headhunter*, she is disguised as the poet Amy, the model of the civilized human being. Margaret Atwood wrote of her: "Over [the] years she created, in a remarkably short time, a complete and diverse poetic universe and a powerful and unique voice, by turns playful, extravagant, melancholy, daring and profound."

MacEwen left us her last words in the last poem of *Afterworlds* and they are words of defiant celebration. They are her testament and legacy:

I hurl
Breathless poems against my lord Death, send these
words, these words
Careening into the beautiful darkness.

Rosemary Sullivan
September, 2007

THE DRUNKEN CLOCK

THE RISING FIRE

1961 · 1963

Certain Flowers

some unthinking god
threw me cold violets last morning
when the rain was a prince in the garden.

said: here, define a certain fear in flowers,
chalk out quickly the peril of beauty,

said softly this, as I worried private light
among the blooms
and stretched a half-winged bird of verse
to band the prince, the bloodless blossoms.

some unthinking god
is made of towering flowers; his eye
in the tall blue tulip sky,
a profound petal there; I arrest its blooming.

I want the flowers beheaded,
the garden sink,
the rain deny its claim to princedom there

and stand in a garden of void
applauding, tracing the biographies
of brief past flowers, capturing the moment of bloom
in a cage of my own sunlight

The Drunken Clock

The bells ring more than sunday; eve,
orchards and high wishes meet the bells
with grace and speed. The staggered
clocks only cousin the bells; after
the timed food, the urgent breakfasts,
we lean to other seasons. Season

of the first temple
of a basic babel
of sumer
of meek amoeba

Clocks count forward with craze, but
bells count backwards in sober grace.
Tell us, in the high minute after they
sing, where the temple is; where
the bell's beat breaks all our hour-
glasses; where the jungled flesh
is tied, bloodroots.

The Breakfast

under the knuckles of the warlord sun how long do we have
how long do we have, you ask, in the vast magenta wastes
of the morning world when the bone buckles under for war
when the bone intersects as tangents in the district of the sun
centipedes and infidels; snakes and the absence of doves?

a breakfast hysteria; perhaps you have felt it,
the weight of the food you eat, the end of the meal coming
before you lift the spoon; or eat only apples
to improvise an eden. or forget the end takes place
in each step of your function.

look, the spoon is lifted halfway through invisible tables
of dangerous logarithms in the abstract morning spaces;
come, come – eat leviathans in the breakfast wastelands
eat bestiaries and marine zoos and apples and aviaries.
by eating the world you may enclose it.

seek simplicities; the fingerprints of the sun only
and the fingernail of the moon duplicating you in your body,
the cosmos fits your measures; has no ending;

place one hand before the sun and make it smaller,
hold the spoon in your hand up to the sky
and marvel at its relative size; comfort yourself
with the measures of a momentary breakfast table.

ah lord sun
ah terrible atomic breakfast
ah twilight of purple fallout
ah last deck of evening cards—
deal, infidel, the night is indeed difficult.

The Mountain: A Study in Relative Realities

the staccato from the gut
like sunset guns, the way we stutter
cryptic causalities and command queer reasons
for mountains based on smashed senses— eyes
like screens, ears like blocked harbours, skulls
like tonal caves which echo altogether too much
and hearts like red whales behind the fishbone ribs
which are boorish and stupid and fly our brains
like kites

is too much. Ah
in our weird apocalyptic sceneries, whimsies
and filigreed senses define little after all;
a mountain is an inviolate triangle in an offhand
way, vaguely difficult to handle in a manual
sense, but our sunset faces are sweet landscapes
with rosy retinae and receptive nostrils and
it is too soon to think of halfway vision and
the questions of perception of an inverted people
etcetera.

The mountain...say
imagine we could double it or make an octave
of mountain or generally manipulate things concave
or convex or whatever, an amusing distraction
like war or dominoes, though somewhere the point
is lost. But now you watch me through your sunset

senses for you expected a poem and prose is suggested.
O men mouthing staccato causalities, O women with
queer cryptic reasons for all things— I grant
it is difficult in these equivocal Canadian sunsets
to imagine that through your senses you do indeed
invent the mountain.
Anyhow, absurd,
but it does serve literature.
Anyone for tea before the night falls?

Universe And

something we know of mountains
and craters within craters—
big braille under a blind God's hands

space. our timorous temples turn
inward, our introverted temples
turn, as the flyer hoists our vision higher

on earth, the machines of our myth
grind down, grind slowly now, rusting
the wheels of human sense

we drink white milk while
high galactic fields open
their floodgates   open

and the terrible laughter of our children
is heard in that pocket, that
high white place above our thunder

Universe And: The Electric Garden

the protons and the neutrons move, gardener,
sire their sons, spirals of sense,
and servant their planets,
their negative pebbles
in a pool of moons; electrons like
mad bees
          circle;
                the nuclei reach out
to harness them;
                will of the sun reach out,
strap earth, strap moon, slowly excite
other stars, set, set the sweet fanatic pace
going;
          telescopes turn inward, bend down.

in our gardens are electric roses
which spark, push light, push fuchsia
in flailing grass

and spines of long magnetic seas cloy…
rake their depths for dust; all holds;
the spines hold the elemental jelly
of the sea's flesh there…

I walk warily through
my electric garden

The Death and Agony of the Butterfly

a monarch beat its velvet brain
against the light, against
the cold light, I
thought of you.

dance you, dance
you bitch
against the light against
the cold light, that's
what you said.

always behind me, always
behind me is
your violent music, beat
until the butterfly's velvet brain
is dead

dance you, dance
you bitch, I
love you against
the light against
the cold light, always
behind me is
your violent music.

The Magician: Three Themes

One: The Magician

odd that the people want to own you
and produce you like a black poodle
at fatal tea-parties where their blood crowds
up in the thunder of the afternoon,
inside their houses, in the fatal rooms
of their faith and dark doubting.
pull the shades of their windows
and give them what they want which is
the brilliance of their own darkness,
their shrouded blood hooked out
on gleaming master fisherman's wires
for the dance of the ultimate arteries
and the brain's calypso and the shifting
of their minds' hard shadows.

Two: The Magician as Man

but it's irksome spending whole afternoons
producing pearly rabbits
for the lettuce-patches of any house
when my real love is the mind
moving as sailboat through the days,
the whiteness and the freedom of it.

Three: The Magician as Christ

yet like penicillin from a mould
his pretense breeds wonder
at the throat of their belief
like fingers or a strange bacteria
holds the hard mind screaming;
the crust and the context of his act
holds in bright hypnosis
the white of their brains
and the dark of their veins, how
much of him is theirs, how much of him
do they re-create in the vast thunderous churches
of their need...

The Dimensions of a Tiger

the cat in the grass lengthens—
and your tendons reach widely
into seasons of wind and deltas—
you are suddenly aware that
you have no boundaries, that
you are a field with no fences.

hollyhock and frolic, you
are the width of wind and voices
until something, a microscopic irony
like laughter breaking from windows
or a diminutive rain shrinks you
and the cat in the grass curls under.

Morning Laughter

To my mother, Elsie MacEwen

umbilical I lumbered
trailing long seed, unwombed
to the giant vagina, unarmed,
no sprung Athene
—cry, cry in the sudden salt
of the big room, world
—I uncurled plastic limbs of senses,
freed the crashing course of menses,
—hurled

I hurled the young tongue's spit
for a common coming, a genesis
sans trumpets and myrrh, rejected
whatever seed in love's inside
fought and formed me from
an exodus of semen come
for the dream of Gwen,
the small one,
whose first salt scream
heralded more and borrowed excellence.

years have tied the sweet cord;
morning laughter, ships of daughter
and of mother move together
in clumsy grace:
you look to a roof of brass clouds
crash loud as the known world knows us;

and each motion's intrinsic as I reach
beyond roofs for a clutch of that first seed.

wary we speak from a fringe of meanings,
circle and pat-a-cake in cat-paw diplomacy,
each hope hoisted to a veined rainbow,
our common denominator, whose colours
are all blood and bone,

wary we speak from a fringe of meanings,
each tongue censored with love and its
cat-paw circling
    ,now foetal in the world's wide womb
    ,now known in my own rebellious belly
     the stuff to people further days
    ,now forced by some grim reason
     to hark down the bonds of the blood
    ,can still remember from that womb walking,
     sideways out of that womb,
     glorious from that womb, bent and insolent.

morning laughter with your young daughter—
smile at the pen she picks, armed to bring light
into terrible focus
and the paper builds worlds but makes
no prodigal...

who would erase the scribbled slate
of gone years, their jumbled algebra,
their rude designs

junked under a rainbow, all blood and bone
that links the mother and the morning daughter—
and acknowledge now, armed and still insolent
that what is housed in the fragile skull
light or learning or verbal innocence—
grows from the woman somehow who housed the whole
body,
who first fed the vessels, the flesh and the sense.

For Alick MacEwan: d. 1960

what we have left behind us in the fathering clay
the finishing bed where the veins flow grey
in the grave unequivocal, is little, redundancy.

long, long beneath the morning moon of our halfway
vision, our wrong repent repeats, stalls
the noon coming, is wrong recalling.

(stolen stolen by the thieves of gravity,
the inverse womb, the inward worm, etc.
O God forgive us these, etc.)

but say you chase life the way you chase
the sunset in grey jets on sunday still
though an organist's veins are opening

for the last warm music; you
were classic somewhere in Canada on sunday
touching trees where old apples fall and birds occur—

(give us that particular cruelty necessary
to take it, your life, a second time, it is
time to speak the truth, it is time to speak,
it is time)

The Catalogues of Memory

1.

now in our distorted distances
the ignorant ships
kiss
and pass

love we have learned nothing
we have learned
nothing
not in the slated nights
not in the chalkboard cities

Jesus, Nietzsche, call them
and they will not come for you
though your hair is on fire
from the brain beneath it burning

love we have learned nothing
we have learned
nothing
not on the gold island
not on the washed beaches

we were two ships of burning glass
we were two ships of burning glass

now in our distorted distances
the ignorant ships
kiss
and pass

2.

endangered
you
the strokes of the sun were
lashes to your lips your
brow
beauty burning in
the fires of your room

ah what do I speak
I with pencils
what do I speak
who love you
under fire and churches
in snow
in rainlight
even behind the seasons

sunday somewhere you were
red and gold on beaches
disturbed with gulls
and steamers

monday somewhere you were
gay among ruins
old stone the fake
architecture of Kingsmere
dancing the colours were
Fall the colours fell
into your hair into
your brow etc.

ah who am I with pencils
who love you
behind reason
behind the poem
even behind the seasons
defining as the poem pillages
reason, you who defy the reasons
of poetry, you endangered
by your own images

3.

your hand on my left breast
perhaps, or the ankles
staying; the genitals like tears;
your eyes wide with fear.
the attack.
lions...the lean loins of them,
we were ships, we were lions, we

were delicate with our images,
we were man in a blind man's vision
and our name was adam and we had no home.

always always was your face moving
before the ships before the buildings,
a crescent leaning, the conscience
of the flesh.

now it is winter; heed, heed
I say, heed
the speech of your hands.
feet, feet, I say,
move swiftly,
leave
no track

The Choice

and so we have a choice of several deaths.

death one, the catapult far-flung wish
from the stomach or the skullcave
shot like a bat out of belfries
or various hells, like a horse
through a landscape of cardboard
calendars.

death two, it is lovely, it is lovely
the second death, you
do not even know it, you
just fold up on a subway
like yesterday's newspaper
until someone picks you up
not bothering to read you.

death three, it is dirty, it is dirty
the third death because
you plan it. it offends
people, it is offensive, a car
from a cliff, a hole behind
the eyes, a drug dream.

and so we have a choice of several deaths
and that in itself is a consolation.
so go to it love, go to it:

the red of the flower your fingers are holding,
the green in the speech of your mouth;
drive it, drive the horse through landscapes
like calendars of cardboard, or nonsense mosaics
for we are great statements in our days

and on the basis of that we can expect small audiences.

The Pied Piper

was he only
I ask you
a magnet, radical
and yellow in their towns
or a gay science, I ask
you, was he only a
momentary messiah, was
he only these?

children still wait
for the absurd
red and yellow music; they
have not forgotten
him tho you wish
they would

forget, always forget
the piper, the pied
piper, the red and yellow
piper. O gentlemen,
in your cities of rats
someone hears a gentle music,
someone laughs.

JULIAN THE MAGICIAN

TERROR AND EREBUS

1963 · 1964

from the Introduction to
JULIAN THE MAGICIAN

This compelling first novel by 22-year-old Gwendolyn MacEwen is a brilliant tour de force. *Although the story is placed in no particular century or country, Julian as magician embodies contemporary concerns of the human condition.*

Momentarily each of us can glimpse our wild beauty in sudden intense lights of self-recognition. But only momentarily. We sleep and guard ourselves. But for Julian, the magician, these lights never go out. For him there is no alternative to consciousness. Consumed by his insights into paralleling the deeds of an earlier "magician," Julian is ultimately begging for his own crucifixion – the supreme parallel.

For the unwitting participants in the passion of Julian, the questions raised are less simply answered. And finally, the question is posed – who was Julian and who was nearest to the truth about him?

ONE / THE BAPTISM

Bulls up out of their rushes, bats' wings, bulls up out of rushes, bats' wings, bulls' blood!...

Absurd, yes – it sounded like a skipping-rope chant of devils; yet it sounded back and forth through Julian's covered ears – antiphonal, riotous, a sing-song of gallumphing spooks, who, when he stole a backward glance, looked just like the people, the townsfolk. Were they shouting it? No, they were clapping, yes – and waving their arms like windmills for him to come back. Somehow their collective shouts had merged in his mind, taken on regular syllables...

Bulls up out of rushes, bats' wings, bulls' blood...

The performance had been good, then. Too good. He'd had to slip out the back way to avoid that sea of bodies that was folding itself up onto the stage, ready to crush him with its love, its hideous worship. It occurred to him that they thought he was divine. Well, they were simple people with brains about the size of the seeds they planted in their fields; they were entitled to their hysteria. Still, when he had felt that post-performance chill, knew in a moment they would be upon him, fingering his robes and clasping his wrist, he had gathered up his money and obscured his mouth with his collar as in a coming sickness – dipped and turned; escaped.

And the people had pushed in, covered the area where he had been standing, circling, suddenly aware of his absence. Some had left; others had remained in the hope that he would return. A young boy guarded the entrance to Julian's wagon, but no one would have entered; no one would have thought to violate those sacred grounds.

"Refuge?" remarked Anya in amusement. "Refuge again?" asked Anya, her big legs straddled between table and oven, her tongue cluck-clucking between the spaces in her teeth.

"Only for a few minutes," Julian said, bunching up his long skirts to sit down.

"I knew you were in the town," she said as she worried the loaf out of the oven, "but I didn't come. Deliberately didn't, I admit, my dear nephew… your fame overcomes me; I prefer to stay in my happy humble home than be recognized as a blood-relative to such greatness…"

"Bless you for it." Julian's forehead folded; then brightened. "O that bread! Admit you use mandrake in it! Admit it!"

"Pooh."

"It's been a long time, Anya… I haven't had a chance to come. I've been touring the countryside. The people…"

"I know. The people worship you," said Anya, setting down the quivering loaf in front of him and sinking in a chair beside it.

"And what's in that fat brain of yours, now? You only look at me like that when you want to make some comment."

"My fat brain has its advantages. Well-padded. It tells me that the people as well as worshipping you – frighten you." She sliced the bread viciously.

Julian wiped some blond hair back from his brow as though it clouded his brain. "They *believe* me," he said after a time, his face twisting into a question mark. "Give me the end of the loaf, Anya… with lots of crust…"

"And you question their belief? This is proof of the excellence of your craft, my boy! It's like my bread. Here," she said, handing him a slice.

"It is not that simple. Bread is not magic."

"Magic is your bread, nevertheless, Julian. Keep to the essentials, I tell you. Your art is sharpened as fine as this blade…"

He tried to eat away her voice with the bread. A good woman – but altogether too basic, too solid, unwilling to see any of the marginal horrors of his profession. She congratulated him on the success he had attained. He did not want congratulations. He came to her to be able to sit and be sane for a while, and be in a silent sane place with the hysterical audience far away, brewing around his caravan like drunken ants; muted.

"And the world's only blond magician!" she went on, inspired by her bread. "No wonder they love you, eh?"

"True. I don't blacken myself... probably the only legitimate part of my act, after all..."

"Yes, but your face, Julian! That's it! You have the features of a gypsy... all that with blond hair!"

"You forget I am a bastard, my dear aunt. My hair was your sister's birthright, and my features were the gift of her lover."

"We don't talk about that now." Anya cut more bread.

"So be it. Yet I must credit that dirty little gypsy – I probably got my talents from him..."

"Julian!"

"A tease, Anya!" Julian was suddenly in good humour. "My dear old fat-brained aunt – I am the servant of the King of Darkness!"

"Fish's wings! The country's full of kings of darkness. Your heart is as gold as your hair, my boy, and your art is devoid of any evil... it's a balm, not a poison."

"Your size excels your wisdom, Anya... but thanks for the bread." He began to leave, his cape wrapped tightly about the shoulders; it was cold, late winter.

"You're still the greatest magician since—"

"I know who since. Good-bye, Anya..."

"Since who, damn you? No Polish magician anyway..."

"Not Polish..." Julian's voice trailed through the door in a muted mumble. "Nazarene..." he murmured.

But Anya had not heard. She shunted from table to oven, cluck-clucking between the holes in her teeth.

The night was altogether too cold. A shame he couldn't manipulate natural elements as he could manipulate human logic and belief. Ancient magicians had a fine time – making the sun rise, inducing rain, assuring the appearance of the moon – but now the duties were more varied and uncertain, success hinged on the more doubtful aspects of human credulity. If success did not come, the magic-maker could sigh for the plight of the human race, its loss of mystical dignity and his loss of money; if success came, the magic-maker could take it with delicacy and restraint; keeping a good eye on practicalities. Or he could double under the weight of his people's devotion if he were an unusually sincere magician with super-respect for his craft. And fear for its real power.

Julian's shoulders were weighted. They were slim like the rest of him, slim and subtle. His wrists were quick, almost with a will of their own, quick and blue-veined. Only his mind excelled their speed.

"You can induce belief..." his old teacher had said when he was still a boy, serving a magician's apprenticeship. "Suspended logic... there's your genius. You can suspend logic like a whale on a thread..."

Julian remembered the words too clearly – his old teacher had been the first to prostrate himself before the blond boy with the gypsy's features. He had had no contemporaries; he had been delicately avoided by them, immersing himself in demonical literature from the age of ten – Boehme first, then back to Magnus in alchemy, Paracelsus and the rest. Alchemy began to bore him – science owed it a vast debt, yes – and science had become the big sister, too big now to allow anyone to make advances towards her bastard kin. He abandoned this line and fell into philosophy; emerged later sobered, but still unsatisfied. The human element wasn't there as he wished it. The human element. Myth. Folklore. Bible. Kabbalah. The Gnostics. The mystical Christ…

Here he found fancy parallels for his own ostracism – a self-imposed one. "Take heed, children, for the future of his company, for he is a sorcerer," said the Arabic Gospel of the Infancy. "Shun and avoid him, and from henceforth never play with him…" so said the mothers to their children of the questionable Christ, so said the written mothers. Julian absorbed it all in great bulk; his young mouth watered. He had the means now – all he needed was the practical apprenticeship, and this he got. He was a born magician.

But the sorcerer's real art is obscured under the weight of action and reaction, play and response – this he learned quickly enough. The art becomes the means of inducing the state of suspended logic – whale on a thread, the teacher had said. The art was indirect, the magic a front, the art a frame.

"Yes, yes, yes… but the shadow of the greatest magician moves behind me. O, the shadow of the greatest magician moves behind me," he chanted to the wind at his face as he walked back to the wagons. "They believe me – so? Why equate myself with a master in my craft? Why equate myself at all?"

Still, his greatest tour de force was the clay sparrows. The fifth-century Gospel of Pseudo-Matthew had it – a delightful story of the mystical Christ, where Jesus playing with children at the Jordan made sdeven pools of clay and passages to bring the water. One of the children shut the passages. "Woe unto thee, thou son of death, thou son of Satan" cried the Christ, and immediately the boy died. The boy's parents, grieved, informed Mary and Joseph. The Christ, not wanting to worry his mother, gave the dead boy a swift kick to the buttocks, saying "Rise, thou son of iniquity." After this, he took clay from the seven pools and fashioned twelve sparrows. Clay sparrows. "Fly!" he implored, picking them up in his hands. "Fly through all the earth and live!"

Julian thanked the mystical Christ for supplying him with his most successful trick – clay and wing, clay and sparrow. No one knew where Julian hid the birds, and even those who had seen the trick performed a dozen times, still watched in vain for the subtle twist of wrist, the obscure something that would expose the method; none found it – sparrows flew from the clay, that was all.

The magician himself began to wonder.

It was a mile back to the wagons; the river was coated in thick ice. The low current was killed under the collar of late winter solidification; the current shackled…

"Still, I only use two birds in my act," the magician thought on.

The river current was choked under the collar of ice. The magician's craft was obscured under the –

"Of course, the more scientific types," Julian thought, "weren't at all hampered by exterior impositions. Galen, Vitruvius perhaps… Hero perhaps, who knows? The scientific outlook… pooh pooh," he added, cancelling the idea. "Pooh pooh and bulls rushing out of their rushes…"

The river was not allowed to flow under the collar of ice blocking its throat-pulse…

Much later the boy still stood, guarding the entrance to the magician's wagon. He straightened, smoothed his black hair at Julian's approach. Apprentice, guard of wagon, maker of meal, leader of horse, counter of money and assistant of act, Peter was

Greek, Peter was prime worshipper of the blond magician in black.

"Eat, sir," he said with an embarrassing shrillness in his voice. "Tomorrow is the big trick—"

"I ate, Peter," the magician answered, wishing somehow that the boy weren't there. Idolization was to be expected from someone like Peter, but it brought curious goose-bumps to the roots of his bright hair. Julian pushed aside the canvas flap and entered the wagon.

Peter was disappointed; he enjoyed watching the magician eat, or drink, or get dressed – any of the things that earthly people take for granted... with Julian all this dissolved into ritual, fascinating to watch. "Soup?" he asked hopefully, sadly, jumping into the wagon behind him.

"Perhaps," Julian thought, "I should urinate on him. Or vomit in full view to convince him I'm human." Peter would never be a magician until he learned to accept the essentials. He couldn't impress this fact upon the boy verbally, for Peter would have answered, "Mister Julian, sir – you are the greatest of them all; your greatness sets you upon another plane," and smiled his thin smile, and so it would have gone. So the magician pulled out a bottle of brandy and took it to bed with him as though it were a woman, lovingly; drank, slept, dreamed innocent alcohol dreams as the dreamy boy assistant up front scrambled the horses over the winter night and the supply wagon brought up the rear.

TERROR AND EREBUS

The Speakers

RASMUSSEN

FRANKLIN

CROZIER

QAQORTINGNEQ

(*Roaring wind which fades out to Rasmussen*)

RASMUSSEN:

King William Island... latitude unmentionable.
But I'm not the first here.
They preceded me, they marked the way
with bones
White as the ice is, whiter maybe,
The white of death,
of purity...

But it was almost a century ago
And sometimes I find their bodies
Like shattered compasses, like sciences
Gone mad, pointing in a hundred directions
at once—
The last whirling graph of their agony.
How could they know what I now know,
A century later, my pockets stuffed with
comfortable maps—
That this was, after all, an island,
That the ice can camouflage the straits
And drive men into false channels,

Drive men
How could they know, even stand back and see
The nature of the place they stood on,
When no man can, no man knows where he stands
Until he leaves his place, looks back
and knows.

Ah, Franklin! I would like to find you
Now, your body spread-eagled like a star,
A human constellation in the snow.
        The earth insists
There is but one geography, but then
There is another still—
The complex, crushed geography of men.
You carried all maps within you;
Land masses moved in relation to
        you—
As though you created the Passage
By willing it to be.
        Ah, Franklin!
To follow you one does not need geography.
At least not totally, but more of that
Instrumental knowledge the bones have,
Their limits, their measurings.
The eye creates the horizon,
The ear invents the wind,
The hand reaching out from a parka sleeve
By touch demands that the touched thing
        be.

(*Music and more wind sound effects, fade out*)

So I've followed you here
Like a dozen others, looking for relics
        of your ships, your men.
Here to this awful monastery
        where you, where Crozier died,
        and all the men with you died,

Seeking a passage from imagination to
        reality,
Seeking a passage from land to land
        by sea.

Now in the arctic night
I can almost suppose you did not die,
But are somewhere walking between
The icons of ice, pensively
        like a priest,
Wrapped in the cold holiness of snow,
        of your own memory...

(*Music bridge to Franklin, wind sound effects*)

FRANKLIN:

I brought them here, a hundred and twenty-nine men,
Led them into this bottleneck,
This white asylum.
I chose the wrong channel and
The ice folded in around us,
Gnashing its jaws, folded in
        around us...

The ice clamps and will not open.
For a year it has not opened
Though we bash against it
Like lunatics at padded walls.

My ships, the *Terror*, the *Erebus*
Are learning the meanings of their
names.
What madman christened them
The ships of Terror and of Hell?
In open sea they did four knots;
Here, they rot and cannot move at all.

Another winter in the ice,
The second one for us, folds in.
Latitude 70 N. November 25, 1846.
The sun has vanished.

(*Music, etc.*)

RASMUSSEN:

Nothing then but to sit out the darkness,
The second sterile year,
and wait for spring
And pray the straits would crack
Open, and the dash begin again;
Pray you could drive the ships
Through the yielding, melting floes,
drive and press on down
Into the giant virginal strait of
Victoria.
But perhaps she might not yield,
She might not let you enter,
but might grip

And hold you crushed forever in her stubborn
    loins,
    her horrible house,
Her white asylum in an ugly marriage.

(*Music, etc.*)

FRANKLIN:

I told him, I told Crozier
The spring is coming, but it's wrong
    somehow.
Even in summer the ice may not open,
It may not open.
Some of the men have scurvy, Crozier...
    Their faces, the sick ones,
    their faces reflect their minds.
I can read the disease in their souls.
It's a mildewed chart
On their flesh.
    But this is no place
To talk of souls; here
The soul becomes the flesh.

(*Sighs*)

I may have to send men on foot
To where the passage is,
To prove it, to prove it is there,
That Simpson joins Victoria,

That there is a meaning, a pattern
        imposed on this chaos,
A conjunction of waters,
        a kind of meaning
Even here, even in this place...

RASMUSSEN:

A kind of meaning, even here,
Even in this place.
        Yes, yes,
We are men, we demand
That the world be logical, don't we?

But eight of your men went overland
        and saw it, proved it,
Proved the waters found each other
        as you said,
Saw the one— flowing into the other,
Saw the conjunction, the synthesis
        of faith, there
In the white metallic cold.

And returned to tell you, Franklin,
And found you dying in *Erebus*,
In the hell
        of your body,
The last ship of your senses.

        June 11, 1847...

(*Music and sound effect bridge*)

RASMUSSEN:

Crozier took command,
A scientist, understanding magnetism,
the pull of elements, but
The laws which attract and as easily repel
Could not pull him from the hell
of his science.

Crozier, what laws govern
This final tug of war
between life and death,
The human polarities…?
What laws govern these?
The ice
Is its own argument.

(*Music bridge*)

CROZIER:

It is September, the end of summer…

(*Laughs briefly, bitterly*)

Summer there was no summer…
Funny how you go on using
the same old terms

Even when they've lost all meaning.

Two summers, and the ice has not melted.
Has the globe tipped? The axis slipped?
Is there no sense of season
Anywhere?

September 1847.
We await our *third* winter in the ice.

(On the word third *a chilling sound effect)*

RASMUSSEN:

But the ice, wasn't it drifting south
Itself, like a ship, a ship within a
Ship?

CROZIER:

The ice is drifting south, but
not fast enough.
It has time, it has more time than we
have time;
It has eternity to drift south.
Ice doesn't eat, doesn't get scurvy,
Doesn't die, like my men are dying.

(*Music to suggest a time lapse*)

CROZIER:

April 1848. The winter is over.
Supplies to last three months only.
We are leaving the ships for good.

RASMUSSEN:

You went overland, then.
Overland, an ironic word...
How can you call this land?
    It's the white teeth
Of a giant saw,
        and men crawl through it
Like ants through an upright comb.
Overland. You set out from the ships
In a kind of horrible birth,
        a forced expulsion
From those two wombs, solid at least,
Three-dimensional, smelling of wood
And metal and familiar things.

Overland...

(*Music bridge*)

CROZIER:

April 21, 1848. Good Friday.
Our last day in the ships.

We pray, we sing hymns, there
        is nothing else to do.
We are all of us crucified
        before an ugly Easter.
Civilization… six hundred and seventy miles away.

(On the words six hundred and seventy miles away *more chilling sound effects)*

CROZIER:

A hundred and five men left. Three months' supplies.
Our Father who art in heaven,
Hallowed be thy name…
        Six hundred and seventy miles to civilization,
Three months' supplies, a hundred and five men…
Give us this day our daily bread
And forgive us…
        scurvy among the men.
        We leave ship tomorrow.
Thy kingdom come, thy will be done…
        Six hundred and seventy miles to
        civilization…
For Thine is the kingdom, and the Power,
And the Glory…
Our Father
Our Father
Our Father

RASMUSSEN:

April 25, 1848. *HMS Terror* and
Erebus were deserted, having been beset
since the 12th of September 1846.
The officers and crew consisting of a hundred and five
souls under the command of Captain F.R.
Crozier landed here.
The total loss by deaths in the Expedition
has been to this date nine officers and
fifteen men.
So you pushed on, and sun and snow,
        that marriage of agonizing light
Assailed you.

(*Music bridge*)

CROZIER:

In the beginning God made the light
And saw that it was good...
        the light...
        and saw that it was good...

(*Eerie music*)

My men fall back, blinded,
        clutching their scorched eyes!
Who ever said that Hell was darkness?

What fool said that light was good
    and darkness evil?
In extremes, all things reverse themselves;
In extremes there are no opposites.

RASMUSSEN:

The naked eye dilates, shrinks,
Goes mad, cannot save itself.
You didn't even have those wooden slits
The eskimos wore
    to censor the sun,
    to select as much light
As the eye can bear.
Some science could have tamed the light
For you,
    not hope, not prayer—
But pairs of simple wooden slits,
Only those, only those ridiculous
    instruments
You need to keep the cosmos out.
I share your irony, Crozier,
That, and your despair…

CROZIER:

(*Breathing heavily while speaking*)

To select what we will and will not see,
To keep the cosmos out with layers of cloth

and strips of leather—
That's man, I suppose,
an arrogant beast. Whether
He is right or wrong is—

O Hell! Look, Lord, look how
They fall back behind me!

(*Music bridge*)

CROZIER:

I sent thirty men back to the ships,
Thirty good men back to the *Terror*, the *Erebus*
for food, somehow.
We can go blind but we must eat
in the white waste.
Though all our senses fall apart
we must eat
we must still eat...

RASMUSSEN:

Thirty good men.
On the way back all of them but five
died,
Knelt before the sun for the last time
and died,
Knelt like priests in the whiteness
and died,

on their knees, died,
Or stretched straight out,
Or sitting in a brief stop
which never ended,
died.

It does not matter how.
Five made it back to the ships
And there, in the womb, in the
wooden hulls,
died.
Five who could not go back,
Who could not a second time
Bear the birth, the going out,
the expulsion
into pure worlds of ice.

(*Music bridge*)

The men do not return with food.
We push on, we cannot wait here.
The winds wait, the sun waits,
the ice waits, but
We cannot wait here;
to stop is to die
In our tracks,
to freeze like catatonics
In our static houses of bone.

Already we look like statues,
marbled, white.

The flesh and hair bleaches out;
        we are cast in plaster.
The ice cannot bear the flesh of men,
The sun will not tolerate colouring;
        we begin already
To move into the ice, to mimic it.
Our Father who art in heaven,
Our Father
Our Father

(*Music, wind*)

One night we saw Eskimos
And they were afraid;
They gave us a seal,
They ran away at night...

(*More music, wind*)

CROZIER:

(*Slowly*)

We have come two hundred miles from the ships,
We have come two hundred miles.
There are thirty men left.
It is the end, it is
The end...

(*Wind, bridge to*)

RASMUSSEN:

Now there was nothing more to do,
 no notes to write and leave in cairns,
 no measurements to take, no
Readings of any temperatures
 save the inner
Agony of the blood.
Now, Crozier, now you come
To the end of science.

CROZIER:

(*Speaking slowly, painfully*)

We scattered our instruments behind us,
 and left them where they fell
Like pieces of our bodies, like limbs
We no longer had need for;
 we walked on and dropped them,
 compasses, tins, tools, all of them.
Now we come to the end of science…

Now we leave ciphers in the snow,
We leave our instruments in the snow.
It is the end of science.
What magnet do I know of
Which will pull us south…?
 none,
 none but the last inevitable
 one.
Death who draws

Death who reaches out his pulling arms
And draws men in like filings
on paper.

This is the end of science.
We left it behind us,
A graph in the snow, a horrible cipher,
a desperate code.
And the sun cannot read, and the snow
cannot either.

(*Music, etc. suggesting death*)

RASMUSSEN:

No, Crozier, the sun cannot read
And the snow cannot either.
But men can, men like me who come
To find your traces, the pieces
Of your pain scattered in the white
vaults of the snow.
Men like me who come and stand
and learn
The agony your blood learned—
how the body is bleached
And the brain itself turns
a kind of pure, purged
white.

And what happed to the ships—
It hurts to talk of it.
The Eskimo Qaqortingneq

Knows—
        let him tell of it...

(*Wind etc. bridge to* QAQORTINGNEQ, *who speaks slowly, falteringly, with language difficulties*)

QAQORTINGNEQ:

I remember the day
When our fathers found a ship.
They were hunting seals,
And it was spring
And the snow melted around
The holes where the seals breathed.

(*Music*)

Far away on the ice
My fathers saw a strange shape,
A black shape, too great to be seals.
They ran home and told all the men
In the village,
And the next day all came to see
This strange thing...

It was a ship, and they moved closer,
And saw that it was empty,
That it had slept there for a long time.
My fathers had never seen white men,
And my fathers did not know about ships.
They went aboard the great ship

As though into another world,
Understanding nothing;
They cut the lines of the little boat
Which hung from the ship
And it fell broken to the ice;
They found guns in the ship
And did not understand
And they broke the guns
And used them for harpoons...

And they did not understand...

They went into the little houses
On the deck of the ships,
And found dead people in beds
Who had lain there was a long time.
Then they went down, down
Into the hull of the great ship
And it was dark
And they did not understand the dark...

And to make it light they bored a hole
In the side of the ship,
But instead of the light,
The water came in the hole,
And flooded, and sank the ship,
And my fathers ran away,
And they did not understand...

(*Music*)

RASMUSSEN:

And the papers? Franklin's papers?
The ship's logs, the reports?

QAQORTINGNEQ:

Papers, O yes!

The little children found papers
In the great ship,
But they did not understand papers.
They played with them,
They ripped them up,
They threw them into the wind
Like birds…

(*Music*)

RASMUSSEN:

(*Laughing bitterly*)

Maybe they were right—
What would papers mean to them?
cryptic marks, latitudes,
signatures, journals,
diaries of despair,
official reports
Nobody needs to read.

I've seen the real journals
You left us, you Franklin, you Crozier.
I've seen the skulls of your men
        in the snow, their sterile bones
Arranged around cairns like
        compasses,
Marking out all the latitudes
        and longitudes
Of men.

(*Music*)

Now the great passage is open,
The one you dreamed of, Franklin,
And great white ships plough through it
Over and over again,
Packed with cargo and carefree men.
It is as though no one had to prove it
Because the passage was always there.
Or... is it that the way was invented,
Franklin?
        that you cracked the passage open
With the forces of sheer certainty?
        —or is it that you cannot know,
Can never know,
Where the passage lies
Between conjecture and reality...?

(*Music, fade out*)

A BREAKFAST FOR BARBARIANS

1964

A Poetic Introduction to the original collection

These poems arise out of a wilful
hunger, a deep involvement with self
and world, a belief that to live
consciously is holy, while merely to
exist is sacrilege. The barbarian,
living close to his original appetites,
has not lost the capacity for joy;
it is a wilful thing.

Here is a book of poems – or call it a
menu. A breakfast menu, breakfast
being a more profound and sacramental
meal than supper, because after all
it's the first meal; it's the pact
you make with yourself to see the
day through.

I should like to think these poems
have a certain value for what I term
their essential 'optimism,' as opposed
to much of the terribly cynical and
'cool' poetry written today. I write
basically to communicate joy, mystery,
passion…not the joy that naïvely
exists without knowledge of
pain, but that joy which arises out
of and conquers pain. I want to
construct a myth.

A Breakfast for Barbarians

my friends, my sweet barbarians,
there is that hunger which is not for food—
but an eye at the navel turns the appetite
round
with visions of some fabulous sandwich,
the brain's golden breakfast
                                        eaten with beasts
                                        with books on plates

let us make an anthology of recipes,
let us edit for breakfast
our most unspeakable appetites—
let us pool spoons, knives
and all cutlery in a cosmic cuisine,
let us answer hunger
with boiled chimera
and apocalyptic tea,
an arcane salad of spiced bibles,
tossed dictionaries—
                                        (O my barbarians
                                        we will consume our mysteries)

and can we, can we slake the gaping eye of our desires?
we will sit around our hewn wood table
until our hair is long and our eyes are feeble,
eating, my people, O my insatiates,
eating until we are no more able
to jack up the jaws any longer—

to no more complain of the soul's vulgar cavities,
to gaze at each other over the rust-heap of cutlery,
drinking a coffee that takes an eternity—
till, bursting, bleary,
we laugh, barbarians, and rock the universe—
and exclaim to each other over the table
over the table of bones and scrap metal
over the gigantic junk-heaped table:

by God that was a meal

It Rains, You See

Reader, I do not want to complicate the world
but mathematics is tragic, there is pathos in numbers;
it's all over, boys— space is curved,
you are hungry and your hunger multiplies by hundreds.

in your first shuddering temple of chalk
in the slate days you taught numbers
to jive under the complex chewing pencils; you talked
darkly of the multiplying world, and your fingers

hunted for braille like urgent forms.
you go outside and now it rains,
and the rain is teaching itself its own name;
it rains, you see, but Hell it comes down cuneiform.

Strange Breakfast

I have eaten
strange breakfasts
with you.

Insatiate. These breakfasts
have broken the past
of smashed appetites;
that colossal intake
of morning images
has made me insatiate (ah you
and your coloured hungers
who doth enclose my life and my death
in your coffee— friend,
we cannot live too long)

obviously we are preparing for some final feast,
obviously our bellies stretch
for a supreme reason, obviously
we can stomach anything now, anything.

that these breakfasts have broken the past
hungers, hungers that were controlled,
controlled hungers, that these breakfasts
have broken them, that everyone does not wish
executed fish and fried eggs,
that the full belly means only
a further hunger, that we cannot now return
to younger appetites, that we can no longer
eat the bright ancestral food,
that we alone must set all our tables single-handed,

that we alone must account for the grease of our spoons
that we alone must wash our mouths
that we alone must look back and decline
all dinner offers,
that we alone will walk into the city at 9 o'clock
knowing that the others have also eaten
knowing that there is no time to compare the contents
of our bodies in our cities
that we eat and we eat and we know and we know
that machines work faster than the machines of our mouths

is why our breakfasts
get stranger and stranger.

You Cannot Do This

you cannot do this to them, these are my people;
I am not speaking of poetry, I am not speaking of art.
you cannot do this to them, these are my people.
you cannot hack away the horizon in front of their eyes.

the tomb, articulate, will record your doing,
I will record it also, this is not art,
this is a kind of science, a kind of hobby,
a kind of personal vice like coin collecting.

it has something to do with horses
and signet rings and school trophies,
it has something to do with the pride of the loins,
it has something to do with good food and music,
and something to do with power, and dancing.
you cannot do this to them, these are my people.

The Children Are Laughing

It is monday and the children are laughing
The children are laughing; they believe they are princes
They wear no shoes; they believe they are princes
And their filthy kingdom heaves up behind them

The filthy city heaves up behind them
They are older than I am, their feet are shoeless
They have lived a thousand years; the children are laughing
The children are laughing and their death is upon them

I have cried in the city (the children are laughing)
I have worn many colours (the children are laughing)
They are older than I am, their death is upon them
I will wear no shoes when the princes are dying

The Metallic Anatomy

Civilization means that I am hardened at the knees
Yet welded delicate— my mind a sickle, a crescent tool
    Strikes a shrill metallic key—
Some days I am simply a long scream
    Sculptured in metal, incredible.

Some tensile art, precise with joy
Breaks my lines, keens me
    To a tense and resonant thing,
And the vats of boiling gold in my brain
    Harden to shrill and intricate shapes.

Now I tell you Fall on your knees
    Before the quivering girders of your city,
Fall on your beautiful precise knees
    Beneath me in the black streets;
This is not poetry, but clean greed—

There is a sculpture which must be made.
O citizen pose for this image of the city.

The Year of the Iron Mouse

in the Tibetan year 1962 the two criminals
    Draco Krake and Scrofula Upulero
were boozing on Queen Street, these two boys
    just like Tibetan mice boozing
on Queen Street, iron and human this
    Scrof, this Krake, who had done
time in pens and schools and the queer
    prisons of ignorance, but Darrow
detested the sin, not the sinner, I wanted
to tell them, and what crime was comparable
to the crime of Queen Street which was
old and ornate getting torn down into
New and Clean; so Krake and Scrof, I thought
we're on the same side of the law, you and me,
    my typewriter has no brand name,
for instance, and this is a simple qualitative
    difference, we each punch out
our areas of freedom even here, and I don't lie
I added, while they ordered more beer.

god, I thought, as they guzzled the draft,
remember Barabbas who said Pilate old boy
I take what little I need and you loot
    continents, O yes, and days ago
Krake and Scrof were picketing for Lucas
and Turpin who got it anyway, what HAVE
    you got? the tigers of wrath are
wiser than the horses of instruction
always.

later on Scrof fell into a bathtub
and gashed an eyebrow bone, and all night
    there were snores and sirens
on Bay Street, and screaming sceptres
    from the Stock Exchange—
do any of us have a pardon for life
in 1962, the Year of the Iron Mouse?
Once Scrof swallowed a baby mouse, whole,
and washed it down with vodka,
that was the whole truth and nothing but it.

*Poem Improvised Around a First Line**

the smoke in my bedroom which is always burning
worsens you, motorcycle Icarus;
you are black and leathery and lean and
you cannot distinguish between sex and nicotine

anytime, it's all one thing for you—
cigarette, phallus, sacrificial fire—
all part of that grimy flight
on wings axlegreased from Toronto to Buffalo
for the secret beer over the border—

now I long to see you fullblown and black
over Niagara, your bike burning and in full flame
and twisting and pivoting over Niagara
and falling finally into Niagara,
and tourists coming to see your black leather wings
hiss and swirl in the steaming current—

now I long to give up cigarettes
and change the sheets on my carboniferous bed;
O baby, what Hell to be Greek in this country
without wings, but burning anyway

**The first line around which it was improvised has disappeared.*

The Self Assumes

not love, lean and frequent,
but the accurate earth,
a naked landscape, green
yet free of seasons
is a name the violate self assumes
after its violent beginnings

not this complex dance of fire and blood
which burns the night to morning,
these hypnotic feet which turn us
know no end and no returning

but a fish within a brilliant river
whose body separates the dreaming waters
and never touches land
is a name the violate self assumes
as silver winds instruct the swimmer
who swims with neither feet nor hands

O not this double dance which burns the night to morning
and cracks the latitudes of time and sleep
whose lean and frequent fires in their burning
break apart the landscapes of a dream,
but the accurate self which burns, and burning, assumes green.

Between You and Me

Between you and me the Messiah stands
like a white and wild chaperone,
our hands are joined onto his hands
and we cannot go anywhere alone.

I know your body by virtue of his flesh
and your words by virtue of his interpreting tongue
and you know me by the same process
and will know me thus for long and long.

We are very aware of his slightest move
and he records every place we three have been,
we are very aware of his going out,
of his going out and of his coming in.

The Left Hand and Hiroshima

asked once why I fanned my fingers before my eyes
to screen the strange scream of them, I, sinister, replied:
Recently I dropped a bomb upon Hiroshima.

as for the mad dialectics of my tooth-chewed hands
I knew nothing; the left one was responsible and
abominably strong, bombed the flower of Hiroshima.

only because my poems are lies do they earn the right
to be true, like the lie of that left hand at night
in the cockpit of a sad plane trailing God in its wake.

all the left hands of your bodies, your loud thumbs
did accomplice me! men women children at the proud womb,
we have accomplished Hell. Woe Hiroshima...

you have the jekyll hand you have the hyde hand
my people, and you are abominable; but now I am in proud and
in uttering love I occur four-fingered and garbed
in a broken gardener's glove over the barbed
                    garden
                    of Hiroshima...

Poem

the slow striptease of our concepts
    —it is even this which builds us,
for you I would subtract my images
    for the nude truth beneath them

as you, voluptuous, as with mirrors at the loins
    are unclothed piece by piece until
each cloth is slander to your skin and
    nakedness itself is silk across your rising sex

Subliminal

in that sublayer of sense
where there is no time
no differentiation of identities
but co-presents, a static recurrence
(that wolf is stone,
this stone is wolf)

your bones have interlocked
behind my brow
your meanings are absolute
you do not move
but are always moving

in that substratum I hold,
unfold you at random;
your eye is a giant
overfolding me;
your foot is planted
in the marrow of my bone,
today is tomorrow.

vision does not flinch
perspective is not jarred
you do not move
but are always moving

you do not move but are always moving
Christ O Christ no one lives long
along that layer;

I rise to see you planted
in an earth outside me,
moving through time
through the terms of it,
moving through time again
along its shattered latitudes

The Peanut Butter Sandwich

we are dangerous at breakfast, at breakfast we
    investigate the reasons for our myths
viciously, and at breakfast we need no reasons
    for being; we are

solemnly eating our thick sandwiches
    and knowing the highest mysticism
is this courageous breakfast and us at it
    concentrating
    conscious

of our outrageous reality. The sandwich!
    The peanut butter sandwich!
a symbol of itself only, and you beautiful
    across the table, eating.

but caught in this cliché of a breakfast
    and knowing it too, we speak
loudly: 'Feed me some symbolisms!
    I want a dragon sandwich!'

'I am freight train, sea-wind and raspberry jam!'
'I am snow, tiger and peanut butter!'

alas, we have too many myths
    and we know that too. but it is breakfast.
I am with you. care for another?

The Last Breakfast

sometimes the food refuses to be sanctified
and you stand over the table beating your chest
and screaming impotent graces for bacon and eggs
graphic on the plate, arranged in a greasy cipher

aware that your body like a graceful vegetable
refuses to be holy; you stop screaming
grace for the eggs and the unsacred bacon,
you stop screaming and sit down darkly

hypnotized by two fried yellow eggs, by this
altogether kanadian breakfast, realizing
your appetite is jaded and the plate is blue
and the food has become an anathema

the bacon has nothing to say for itself
the whole thing is decidedly insane
but you eat the breakfast because it is there
to be eaten, and as you eat
you delicate barbarian, you think of pigs and chickens,
you think of mammoths and their tons of frozen ancient meat,
you think of dark men running through the earth
on their naked, splendid feet

The Magician

for Raymond Lowe

finally then the hands must play mad parables
finally then, the fingers' genius
wave out what my poems have said;
finally then must the silks occur
                                        plus rabbits
and the big umbrellas be
spun on stage continually.

as you Lowe, in quiet irony
inspire terrible skills of silks
                        or crash scarves vertically
as though miniature brains were held in fingertips
fantastic as of secrecy—

or my art being more a lie anyway
than the lie of these illusions
secreting realities in the twitching silks
or sacred sleeves
                        to twist or tamper them
to come out solid, in cubes or cups—
pull down then
                        silk avalanche of scarves
or play the cosmos on strings of human hair
                        as a wand cracks
and blinds belief and holds it knotted
        like an ugly necklace
        or a hopeless rope—

or you, Lowe, driving a spike through the head of a boy
as though magic were (and is)
a nail of steel to split the skull

                                        in either direction

to believe or not believe
is not the question.

finally then do all my poems become as crazy scarves
issuing from the fingers in a coloured mesh
and you, magician, stand as they fly around you
silent as Houdini who could escape from anything
except the prison of his own flesh.

Manzini: Escape Artist

now there are no bonds except the flesh; listen—
there was this boy, Manzini, stubborn with
guts stood with black tights and a turquoise
leaf across his sex

and smirking while the big
brute tied his neck arms legs, Manzini
naked waist up and white with sweat

struggled. Silent, delinquent, he
was suddenly all teeth and knee, straining slack
and excellent with sweat, inwardly

wondering if Houdini would take as long
as he; fighting time and the drenched
muscular ropes, as though his tendons were worn
on the outside—

as though his own guts were the ropes
encircling him; it was beautiful; it was thursday; listen—
there was this boy, Manzini

finally free, slid as snake from
his own sweet agonized skin, to throw his entrails
white upon the floor
with a cry of victory—

now there are no bonds except the flesh,
but listen, it was thursday, there was this boy,
Manzini—

Appendectomy

it's interesting how you can brag about a scar;
I'm fascinated with mine; it's diagonal and straight,
it suggests great skill, great speed,
it is no longer or shorter than it needs to be.

it is good how it follows my natural symmetry
parallel to the hip, a perfect geometry;
it is not a wound; it is a diagram
drawn correctly, it has no connection with pain.

it's interesting how you can brag about a scar;
nothing in nature is a straight line
except this delightful blasphemy on my belly;
the surgeon was an Indian, and beautiful, and holy.

THE SHADOW-MAKER

THE ARMIES OF THE MOON

1969 · 1972

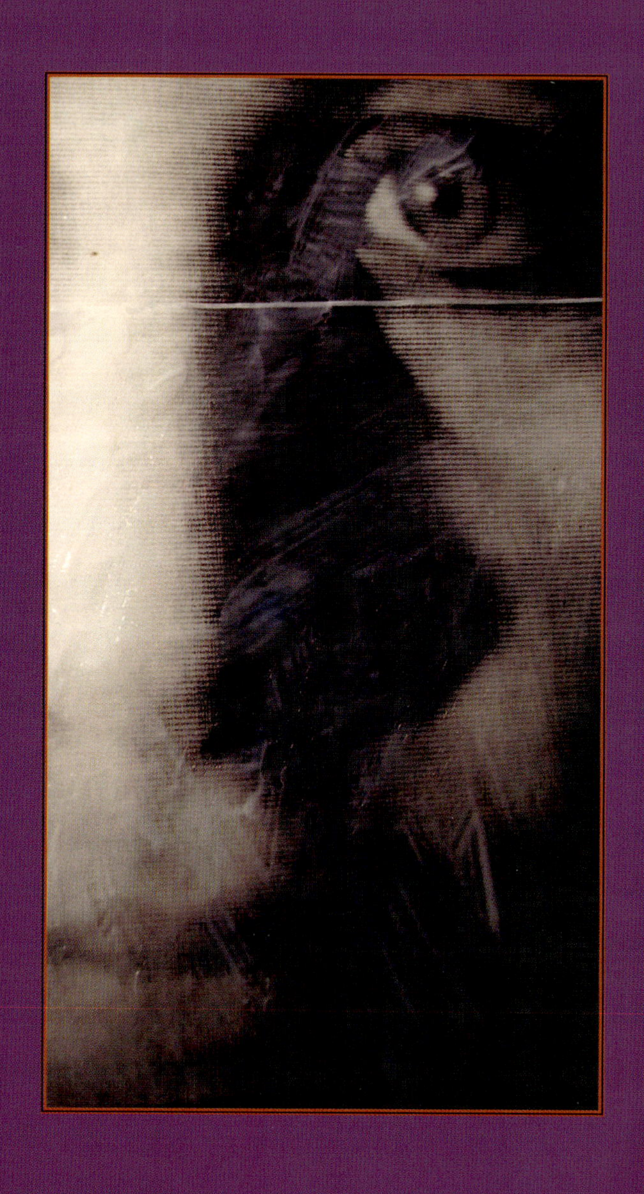

The Red Bird You Wait For

You are waiting for someone to confirm it,
You are waiting for someone to say it plain,
Now we are here and because we are short of time
I will say; I might even speak its name.

It is moving above me, it is burning my heart out,
I have felt it crash through my flesh,
I have spoken to it in a foreign tongue,
I have stroked its neck in the night like a wish.

Its name is the name you have buried in your blood,
Its shape is a gorgeous cast-off velvet cape,
Its eyes are the eyes of your most forbidden lover
And its claws, I tell you its claws are gloved in fire.

You are waiting to hear its name spoken,
You have asked me a thousand times to speak it,
You who have hidden it, cast it off, killed it,
Loved it to death and sung your songs over it.

The red bird you wait for falls with giant wings—
A velvet cape whose royal colour calls us kings
Is the form it takes as, uninvited, it descends,
It is the Power and the Glory forever, Amen.

You Held Out the Light

You held out the light to light my cigarette
But when I leaned down to the flame
It singed my eyebrows and my hair;
Now it is always the same— no matter where
We meet, you burn me.
I must always stop and rub my eyes
And beat the living fire from my hair.

Poem

It is not lost, it is moving forward always,
Shrewd, and huge as thunder, equally dark.
Soft paws kiss its continents, it walks
Between lava avenues, it does not tire.

It is not lost, tell me how can you lose it?
Can you lose the shadow which stalks the sun?
It feeds on mountains, it feeds on seas,
It loves you most when you are most alone.

Do not deny it, do not blaspheme it,
Do not light matches on the dark of its shores.
It will breathe you out, it will recede from you.
What is here, what is with you now, is yours.

The Discovery

do not imagine that the exploration
ends, that she has yielded all her mystery
or that the map you hold
cancels further discovery

I tell you her uncovering takes years,
takes centuries, and when you find her naked
look again,
admit there is something else you cannot name,
a veil, a coating just above the flesh
which you cannot remove by your mere wish

when you see the land naked, look again
(burn your maps, that is not what I mean),
I mean the moment when it seems most plain
is the moment when you must begin again

The Portage

We have travelled far with ourselves
and our names have lengthened;
    we have carried ourselves
on our backs, like canoes
in a strange portage, over trails,
insinuating leaves
and trees dethroned like kings,
    from water-route to
    water-route
seeking the edge, the end,
the coastlines of this land.

On earlier journeys we
were master ocean-goers
going out, and evening always found us
spooning the ocean from our boat,
    and gulls, undiplomatic
    couriers brought us
cryptic messages from shore
till finally we sealords vowed
we'd sail no more.

Now under a numb sky, somber
cumuli weigh us down;
the trees are combed for winter
and bears' tongues have melted
all the honey;
    there is a loud
suggestion of thunder;

subtle drums under
the candid hands of Indians
are trying to tell us
why we have come.

But now we fear movement
and now we dread stillness;
we suspect it was the land
that always moved, not our ships;
we are in sympathy with the fallen
trees; we cannot relate
    the causes of our grief.
We can no more carry
our boats our selves
over these insinuating trails.

Letter to a Future Generation

we did not anticipate you, you bright ones
though some of us saw you kneeling behind our bombs,
we did not fervently grow towards you
for most of us grew backwards
sowing our seed in the black fields of history

avoid monuments, engrave our names beneath your own
for you have consumed our ashes by now
for you have one quiet mighty language by now

do not excavate our cities
to catalogue the objects of our doom
but burn all you find to make yourselves room,
you have no need of archaeology,
your faces are your total history

for us it was necessary to invent a darkness,
to subtract light in order to see,
for us it was certain death to know our names
as they were written in the black books of history

I stand with an animal at my left hand
and a warm, breathing ghost at my right
saying, Remember that this letter was made
for you to burn, that its meaning lies
only in your burning it,
that its lines await your cleansing fire—
understand it only insofar

as that warm ghost at my right hand breathed
down my blood and for a moment wrote the lines
while guns sounded out from a mythical city
and destroyed the times

Dark Pines Under Water

This land like a mirror turns you inward
And you become a forest in a furtive lake;
The dark pines of your mind reach downward,
You dream in the green of your time,
Your memory is a row of sinking pines.

Explorer, you tell yourself this is not what you came for
Although it is good here, and green.
You had meant to move with a kind of largeness,
You had planned a heavy grace, an anguished dream.

But the dark pines of your mind dip deeper
And you are sinking, sinking, sleeper
In an elementary world;
There is something down there and you want it told.

The Shadow-Maker

I have come to possess your darkness, only this.

My legs surround your black, wrestle it
As the flames of day wrestle night
And everywhere you paint the necessary shadows
On my flesh and darken the fibers of my nerve;
Without these shadows I would be
In air one wave of ruinous light
And night with many mouths would close
Around my infinite and sterile curve.

Shadow-maker create me everywhere
Dark spaces (your face is my chosen abyss),
For I said I have come to possess your darkness,
Only this.

The Return

I gave you many names and masks
And longed for you in a hundred forms
And I was warned the masks would fall
And the forms would lose their fame
And I would be left with an empty name

(For that was the way the world went,
For that was the way it had to be,
To grow, and in growing lose you utterly)

But grown, I inherit you, and you
Renew your first and final form in me,
And though some masks have fallen
And many names have vanished back into my pen
Your face bears the birth-marks I recognize in time
You stand before me now, unchanged

(For this is the way it has to be;
To perceive you is an act of faith
Though it is you who have inherited me)

The Hunt

my car goes *behind* the shadows
into the majestic dark of shoes
or cryptic corners where the spirits hide;
for me too this house is not
a mere conspiracy of walls, but
a jungle of eyes, the lost worlds
of the Kalahari, King Solomon's mines.

I know exactly what he's hunting down
day after day in the dark places –
dream creatures with fluorescent eyes
which shine like jewels
in the caves of his awakening.

on the television screen
two ghostly blobs of men dissolve
on the rim of a lunar crater,
and I know exactly what they're hunting down
hour after hour in the seas without water.

now the astronauts are journeying
over the rim of my sleep
and this red-eyed cat dissolves in air;
if you are looking for me now, my Hunter,
you will not find me here.

Hypnos

He lies there in a wilderness of sheets
and his body inhabits strange spaces, oblique
dimensions;
    like the keen emptiness of a child's eye
    it offers me no entry and no alibi.
Horses (I think) charge into
the white night of his sleep.
He celebrates the birthdays of his dreams
and does not know I ponder
how I might join him there.

Yet I fear to even if I could
for in his sleep he is powerful
as a withheld word.

He lies there accomplished and unknown,
his limbs arranged by passion and by art,
a fluid beauty he inhabits all alone.
The dark bird of war is dormant in his loins
and prophets reside in the seeds of his kiss;
    the generations of his mouth are legion
    yet his body is inviolably his.

He may lie, he may live there forever
and I can say nothing of the meaning of this sleeper.

Arcanum One: The Prince

and in the morning the king loved you most
and wrote your name with a sun and a beetle
and a crooked ankh, and in the morning
you wore gold mainly, and the king adorned you
with many more names.

beside fountains, both of you slender
as women, circled and walked together
like sunrays circling water, both of you
slender as women wrote your names with
beetles and with suns, and spoke together
in the golden mornings.

and the king entered your body
into the bracelet of his name
and you became a living syllable
in his golden script, and your body
escaped from me like founting water
all the daylong.

but in the evenings you wrote my name
with a beetle and a moon, and lay upon me
like a long broken necklace which had fallen
from my throat, and the king loved you
most in the morning, and his glamorous love
lay lengthwise along us all the evening.

Arcanum Two: The Conspirator

my brother, you board the narrow boat and the river owns you
over and over; why do you sail like this between your sister
and the distant king? my chamber is full of politics
and hunger. why do you go to him? his chin is thin
and his thighs bulge. why do you go to the king your father?

your boat, your narrow boat goes forth each morning
and snouts of crocodiles worry the water.
why do you go each morning after
our bodies make narrow rivers together?

I know how you plot against the king your father
whose thighs flung you forth as from a salty river;
you will steal the crown which bulges from his head
and mount the thin throne which no one holds forever.

O do not go to the king our father
but stay in this house beside the worried river;
there are a thousand kingdoms yet to conquer
in the narrow nights when we lie together,
and the distant king on his thin and hungry throne
can neither live nor lie nor sing forever.

Arcanum Three: The Death of the Prince

He was employed upon the marble floor
Between the fountain and the pillars.
    They looked for him, the silvery guards
    Sought him all daylong, and my brother
Did not hear them calling through the halls.

And finding him employed upon the marble floor
They fell before him crying: Majesty!
    (Lord, his mouth was terrible
    And his cheek a granite cliff)
And he lifted up his head and smiled.

He was destroyed upon the marble floor
Between the fountain and the pillars
    And I bent over him to call his name,
    His secret name whose syllables were thunder—
Then I took the heavy crown and threw it in the river.

Arcanum Four: The Enbalming

along your body strips of gold unroll
your name which caused a kingdom's fall
and your wrapped ribs, my silent one,
refuse the sun, and down your legs run
legends of the night. in white cloth I wound you
in your final house beside the water
and I know the gates are locked forever,
the gates of light are locked forever
as my loins lock, as the river.

in white cloth bound, and blind
you breathe in death the winds of night
as the sweet stiff corpse of your petrified
sex points upward into heaven
in your tomb beside the river,
though the gates of light are locked forever,
the legs and lips of light are locked forever.

my fingers twice have traced
your name all down your flesh, and they
have dipped its signs in water.
now sleep my blind, my silent brother
as my womb locks, as the river,
your tomb a virgin by jackals sealed
and the gates of light are locked forever.

Arcanum Five: The Prayer

death is a snake on your smashed brow
but still I beg you to get up and go
beyond the drowning river where your crown lies
towards the sighing house of reeds where I
stand waiting in the hollow doorway of eternity.

O brother, from your tomb arise! your bones
are targets in a hunter's eyes, your soul
the naked arrow which he fires.

in the name of our father, by the ring he wore,
come touch this floor with feet that burned
a thousand times the grass between the river
and this fervent house.
as bird arise, as arrow! and tomorrow
let the strips of linen fall.
all your limbs are tombs of sorrow.
I beg you now, my silent brother
to crash those gates which are not locked forever.
O bless and break them ten times over!

Arcanum Six: The Centuries

I waited two millennia in the house beside the river
calling to the north wind many times over,
and feeding doves, and laying fruit beside your tomb
which thieves and beggars stole by night in summer,
and burning prayers and perfume on the hungry altar.
elsewhere slept our mad forgotten father
and the land fell into wretchedness, and later
watersnakes and foreign boats profaned the river.

and sometimes you visited as bird the thirsty bed
where we had lain, and hovered above and said,
"I will come back in better forms than this,
my sister, but the gates are hard to break,
so hard to break you cannot know
and death is like the long sleep after love
when nothing can persuade the limbs to move."

your tired wings were songs among the leaves
and on my thighs you left your shining, unreal seed.

and other centuries I do not try to count
with doves and thieves and moons appeared and went,
with stars that wrote strange warnings in the skies.
the eyes of many kingdoms closed, the palace was defiled
by princes with strange-coloured eyes.

brother, I awaited the end of all the world.

Arcanum Seven: The Return

now as I wear around my neck a necklace
of a million suns, you come
undead, unborn, thou Ghost of the morning!

I notice that you wear our father's ring
but I must say no more
for the bed of ebony and straw
lies like a fallen song upon the floor
where last we left it, broken with love and bare.
the world will loathe our love of salt and fire
and none will let you call me sister here.

see how my body bears the mouthmarks made
in times long past, star-wounds in night unhealed;
since then it was a cave by jackals sealed.
but now my legs are once more cages
for a great far-flying bird, my breasts
small pyramids of love, my mouth
is empty of the dark wine of my waiting.

O tell me all the things you saw,
and call me sister
and bless this bed of ebony and straw.

Arcanum Eight: The Story

"sister, from the gates and fields of night I came
lured by your voice as it spoke my name
over water and fire, and the voice of him
who told me that his sun would burn forever.

"I'll tell you why I went each morning to the river
and sailed towards that old man on the throne.
his seed struggled in my reluctant thighs
and the ring on his hand was stone
and his eyes were the mirrors of the world
and he was the very lord of gold.

"so I went each morning to the king my father.
but all is told, I cannot tell another thing
about how his blood was the birth of my soul
and how with my own hands I killed the king, the king.

"now when the sun is born each day at dawn
I will lie along your body as a boat along a river
and place my soul a blazing ornament upon your breasts
and burn with my bones my name all down your flesh.
sister, by a dark love bound and blind
I touch you now, in this forbidden time
and my white robes of death unwind."

Arcanum Nine: The Rings

I do not adorn you with any more names
for the living ghost of the king our father
hovers forever above our secret bed
like the royal hawk with wings outspread
on whose head the awful sun burns out
the many generations of our dreams.

and we are the end of his ancient line,
your seed a river of arrested time
whose currents bring the cursed crown
forever back to the foot of this bed—
the double crown of those who wear
the kingdoms of heaven and hell on their head.

the royal bird is blind in morning
and its glamorous wings will shade us
till the end of time. but O my brother
will you wear forever that stolen ring
which wounds your hand by night, and why
in your dreams do you go to the king, the king?

KING OF EGYPT, KING OF DREAMS

NOMAN

THE FIRE EATERS

MERMAIDS AND ICONS: A GREEK SUMMER

1971 · 1972 · 1976 · 1978

THE PAPYRUS OF MERITATON

Circa 1549 B.C.

Give me the hands that hold your soul
And I will receive your soul and never die.
Call upon me by name forever and ever
And never shall it sound without reply.

No, Smenkhare, I told no one where I buried you. Would the Nile ever reveal its source? Often from out of the dark deserts of my sleep I cry "*Ifnai, Ifnai, he is mine!*" for in death you are mine as in my own death I am yours.

It is easy to die, easier than I ever would have thought. I simply do not eat; I let my body consume itself bit by bit and burn itself out like a candle. They cannot deny me this privilege; I am a royal person and my last command is to be allowed to die. Oh, there are some who try to talk me out of it – my sister Ankhesenamon, who is queen, and my grandfather, the Vizier Ay. He comes almost every day and pleads with me, but I spit on him, this "Priest of Maat." His face is dark and sullen like the bottom of a pool; his eyes are slanted and his mouth curls downward in a perpetual sneer. I sense there is blood on his hands, but I don't know whose. Sometimes I think it is our father's blood. Today I slapped his mouth (I hate his mouth) and he left my room with his head hanging, like a sick dog.

Tutankhamon struts about his palace in a robe studded with little golden rosettes, playing at his newest game of being king. The Horizon is no more and the royal house dwells once again in the city of Amon. After his coronation the little beast took his revenge upon you, and permitted the priests to close down your mortuary temple and forbid you the privileges of a royal burial. He, like them, did not acknowledge that you were ever king. The servants of Amon confiscated all you possessed; they seized the three golden shrines that were to house your coffin, the little golden coffins for your vital organs, the chairs and couches, the *ka-house* for your statue – everything. They ground out your name from the furnishings and one day they will be used for the tomb of Tutankhamon. May it be soon! May he meet his death in some disgusting ignoble manner that will make people snicker and laugh!

Meanwhile your body lies in the dankest, filthiest hole in the Valley of the West; seven a peasant would shun it as his final house, but in your meagre death, Smenkhare, you are more of a king than the spoiled boy who now sits on the throne.

I feel I am eight years old again, and I am falling, falling onto the magical floor in the palace of the Horizon. My big turquoise ball rolls across the pavement, over the animals and birds, the painted cranes standing one-legged in their painted marshes. It rolls over the flat papyrus thickets, the herons and flamingos and kingfishers and ducks. How I loved that floor – the green zigzags on the plaster, the tall reeds and flat faces of the captives of Khor! I used to sit in the different squares and make fantasies about the occupants. One day I was in the papyrus thicket square, which in itself was not very exciting, but it reminded me of the times my nurse Benremut took me to the riverbank to play among the waterplants, dozing there and having horrible dreams of the ovens of Hell, the lakes of Fire, the Swallowers. Dreams of crocodiles surfacing from the water with the hands of Horus between their teeth – the most honourable death was to fall into the Nile and be devoured by a crocodile – dreams of Isis hovering in the air like a hawk over the corpse of Osiris, taking his seed. I didn't know what that last part meant, but it sounded wonderful, and after all, I couldn't understand all the legends Benremut told me. Father said I had to forget those awful tales, for they had no part in the Teaching. He told Benremut to shut her mouth, which was hard on her, for her mouth was all she had, really. She was never quite the same afterwards; she'd sit all day stringing collars and cursing when she dropped the beads. She'd learned the curses from Ay, who was always willing to share his vocabulary with anybody who was interested.

She couldn't care less about the floor. I couldn't understand how anybody could just walk over it to get somewhere, without getting lost in it, or lying flat out upon it like I did. Flat out, my toes stretching far as the foot of the flamingo, my fingers reaching back to poke out the eye of the Khorian.

I was the Beloved of Aton, and I wore long strands of jewels in my ears and a wide collar of flowers and nothing else. My fingernails were bright silver, and all the hair was shaven from my head except for one sidelock held by a turquoise ring. This drew attention to my long narrow head. All my sisters had long heads too, like our father; he permitted us to wear no headdresses to disguise the elongation of our skulls. It was not an abnormality, he said, but a sign.

I was small and tubular and unripe, and my body was for me a kind of toy, a lithe nut-brown thing with no dark places, no secrets.

The big turquoise ball went plop into the pond and I lay back imagining that I was painted onto the floor. Father would come and be unable to find me; he'd walk all over me and I'd just scream with laughter. Then he'd look down and see that his princess no longer lived in the world of men. They'd bring me my food and I'd still have to continue my writing lessons, but it would all be so much more tolerable. How silly everyone would look – giving advice to the floor, scolding it, taking orders from it! I laughed out loud and Benremut looked up dully. Like her father Ay, she had no sense of humour. She never smiled. She laughed a lot, but that's different.

Then I looked up and saw you standing in the doorway. You were brown and lean and you wore the pleated linen tunic of a young aristocrat. You were confident but not arrogant; you seemed overly serious, always brooding over some secret problem. But you were only eleven then, and the sidelock hadn't yet been shaven from your head. Your eyes were wonderfully clear and large, your features small but well-shaped. And your teeth, when I could see them on the rare occasions of your laughter, were even and white. You were so restrained and controlled, but there were always parts of your body which betrayed you – a flickering muscle in the cheek, a hand clenching and unclenching. Your left eye, more candid and clear than your right…

You stood for a moment absorbed in something, then wandered over to me and sat down on the Khorian's left foot. A small live bird was pulsating in your palm and you held it out to me. "I caught it this morning in the marshes, do you want to hold it?"

you asked. I answered, "I'm a floor, and a floor can't hold anything!" but then I felt rather silly and accepted the tiny throbbing bundle of white feathers. You showed me your new throwstick, painted bright blue and decorated with flowers and *Wedjet* eyes. "The king, your father, gave it to me, it's the same kind as his!" you said proudly. "When I throw it, it's so well glazed that it catches the light and flies like a shiny blue hawk against the sky!" You fondled the weapon and I watched you, proud that you chose to speak to me about such remote boy's business.

"I just clipped this bird on the wing, enough for it to fall," you said, and while its warm vibrant belly nestled in my palm I told you about my father's aviary which was going to be built in the North Palace with hundreds of little niches for nests and long drinking troughs. I asked if you intended giving him the bird, and you replied very emphatically that you'd catch a rare one for him – one he could never find himself. At that moment you reminded me of someone I knew very well, so well that it was impossible to recall.

You looked down at my body. "You have no breasts," you said.

Now I had often watched how grown-up ladies behaved with men, and I replied with what I thought was the proper mixture of coyness and sophistication. True, I was only eight, but in Keme one learns such things very early. "In three years my breasts will start growing, I was told they would. But if you speak to me again about breasts I'll tell Benremut. You may come back in three years and see them, though – if you like." Then I turned sideways and pressed my fists down between my legs in what I thought was an attitude of mature indignation. "You don't have any either!" I cried.

"But I don't want any."

"You have *something else,* and I know all about it."

"And that's another thing you don't have!"

"I don't need one— so there!"

"Well, you look pretty funny without it," you said, staring down at the naked little hump between my legs.

I took the bird and placed it there, to cover my nakedness, but you gently removed it from my lap and held it by the feet while it fluttered and tested its wings.

"When you have breasts," you whispered, "I will come and touch them."

I started to protest but when I saw your mouth pulled back in a wide flashing grin, I forgot what I was going to say and gazed fascinated at the most beautiful teeth I had ever seen. Nevertheless, I vowed to tell my father of your impertinence.

"Keep the bird," you said, "and in three years it will fly away free." You forced it back into my hands, got up from the floor, and passed out through the gates. The blue throwstick still flashed in your hands, catching the afternoon rays of the Aton on its glaze. I stayed a while longer and tried to renew my games, but soon lost interest and found myself musing on how the north harem where you lived was almost exactly opposite my quarters in the royal estate, across the Royal Road. And from the top terrace of my father's garden, where all the trees were, it would be very easy to see.

Then suddenly I was ten, and I watched Father's artisans make my set of coffins. Strange to be a child and look dispassionately upon one's own house of death. Foreigners think that we in the Two Lands love death, but how wrong they are! We hate it and dread it and we furnish ourselves for the great journey well in advance. It is life we love, jealously, painfully, and wish to continue it forever.

They were grinding up lumps of red ochre into a paint crimson as blood. There were three coffins – each to be contained in the other, like three generations, I think; past, present and future. The middle one was made of wood and covered with great sheets of gold foil inlaid with a feather pattern of turquoise and carnelian stones. A long strip of gold ran from the chest to the feet, awaiting the insertion of the signs which would identify me. I watched them lay the gold mask over the wooden face and I stood transfixed with its beauty and wished my own face could be pure gold.

Then I felt something behind me, and turned to see you watching me, your head cocked at a studious angle, your eyes slighting squinting. "I am thirteen today," you announced, and stared at the coffin with its great wings of jewels. You walked around it, your face clouded with some strange trouble.

"What's wrong, don't you like it?" I asked.

"I don't know, don't ask. I think I saw a name on the golden strip."

"*My* name will be on it, and my father's, and the name of the Aton."

"Those were not the names I saw," you said.

We walked down the long path from the palace to the river and the way was lined with shrubs and palms. Father's barge floated on the green water held by mooring stakes to the shore; its dozens of oars languished in the river like tongues, its masts were straight as young men's spines, white sails shivered high above the bright red cabin. Around it were sycamore skiffs, single-sailed boats, a few freight ships waiting to carry out their cargos of coloured glass which the Horizon manufactured. Fishermen, their faces brown as ancient papyrus, sat mending nets by the shore.

"You still have no breasts, Beloved."

"Next year I will. This year I have buds and they hurt me."

"I bet you can't run, then. I've seen girls your age running and they look like they're going to fall apart."

"I can run!" I cried, and to prove it I darted down to the riverbank and collapsed beneath a palm. You sat beside me and drew up your knees to your chin and rocked back and forth. We spoke of the seasons and you told me your favourite month was this one, Hathor, because it was your birthday, because the river receded and the air cooled and the peasants sowed their crops. I told you mine was the first month of the flood, and you replied that that was how it should be, for the river in its inundation was like a woman, while the river receding lean and calm was more like a man. I didn't see the point, but I nodded wisely and told you about the time I found a foreign coin left behind by the Nile; I had washed the mud from it and shown it to my father. But he had thrown it back into the Nile, for there was an image on it which displeased him.

Once again an expression came over your face which reminded me of someone I knew very well.

"What are all your other names?" I asked.

"Names! I have a hundred names!" and then you recited something:

In the Great House and in the House of Fire
On the dark night of the counting of all the years,
On the dark night when months and years are numbered,
O let my name be given back to me!

I asked you what it meant but you said you really didn't know. You found it written in one of the ancient books in the Baou Ra. "But the books in the Baou Ra libraries are forbidden!" I cried.

"Not to me they aren't," you murmured, and your expression told me the matter was closed.

We watched the green heaving river for a long time. The great Nile with its seven mouths, its living pulse, its green death. We argued about its source, for I believed it was born in the Underworld, but you scoffed and called me a child. You had known that was untrue, since the tender age of seven, and since then had lacked all such illusions. You several times got into fistfights with your young friends over it.

"All right, then, where *is* the source?" I asked.

"What do you mean, where is the source? I don't know *that.* I only know it's *a secret of movement, a darkness in daytime.* Wanre told me that."

You were silent a long while, then said suddenly, "Would you like to live long?"

"Father says the Aton determines the length of life. And you?"

"Short, like the wind. I want to burn and die like a thunderbolt, like a flame."

The living river was west; the hollow tombs in the cliffs were east. Between life and death we sat, between the water and the stone we sat, children who did not know the meaning of our own words. We went back to the palace and parted at the gates.

"I understand nothing," you said, and I burst into a fit of nervous laughter (I'd been laughing a lot lately; it had something to do with having hurting buds of breasts and being almost eleven). Then I ran away and left you standing alone. Now when I think of you I do not remember you as a king, but as a boy on his thirteenth birthday saying, *"I understand nothing."* And I did not even know the nothing which you didn't understand. I remember the day I wore a necklace of glass fish and grasshoppers joined by small glass suns, and a palm-leaf basket laughing with flowers hung from my arm. The air was a web of gold as we walked through the gardens of the summer palace of Meru Aton. Ahead of us was my private shrine, surrounded by tiny canals and waterplants, and I told you that yesterday I'd offered a goose and five ripe melons to the god. You trailed along with me beside the gurgling musical canals and said that my father's world was a miniature garden like this one, and that he must begin to look outside, or the weeds would eat their way into his world and destroy it.

"That monstrous!" I cried. "If you were king, what would *you* do?"

"I'd preserve the garden," you said, "I'd make terms with the weeds!"

Just then I spotted a rabbit and went bounding after it behind a bush. I got down on my belly and tried to poke my arm through the little thicket where I saw it disappear, but it got away. I felt you drop softly beside me then.

"Princess, you have breasts. Let me touch them!"

"But Benremut—"

"Is busy watching her reflection in the water..."

Shyly you placed your hand on one breast, then on another. You touched a glass fish on my collar and said you wished you were a fish plunging and dipping into mysterious rivers or swimming about in secret enchanted pools. Just then your finger caught on one of the grasshopper's sharp glass feet and you winced with pain. A drop of blood appeared at the tip. I rolled over and over on the grass laughing at you, but suddenly your young body was flat upon me and your mouth covered my mouth. For a moment I did not breathe or move; then I pushed you away. "She's coming!" I whispered. And we had just enough time to get up from the grass before Benremut reached us.

That night, alone, I caressed the small glass fish. I wanted to touch that secret part of you I'd never seen but only felt when you were upon me, that strong hard part between your legs which was made to dive and swim in dark unknown rivers. Recently my mother had told me I should expect something very soon. She had wept, and I had asked myself, why was Nefertiti weeping, she who was so beautiful, no one in the whole kingdom was half so beautiful, why did my mother weep?

And a week after your fell upon me beneath the bushes of Meru Aton, the red wetness between my thighs told me I had become a woman. The kiss must have made it begin in me, your hard body must have drawn it out.

A month before you became my husband we couldn't encounter each other without stammering and blushing, for the memory of that afternoon in the summer palace loomed up before us golden and red. Now you were eighteen, and I, fifteen. Tiy was dead. My beautiful mother Nefertiti was dead. We were no more children. We knew more was to come for us than a kiss in the bushes or a cut finger from the edge of a glass grasshopper. What would it be like? I asked myself a thousand times but my imagination called up only the most hazy pictures. Behind the haze, though, my blood coursed strong as the Nile in flood, and my blood knew. It would be a new and secret form of night. The Lord of the Atmosphere holds heaven and earth apart, but when Nut descends to lie with Geb, everything becomes dark as it was in the beginning.

On our wedding night after the feasts and dances were over, we were alone in our vast apartments. Two great eunuchs stood in the hall outside our door, guarding, not our privacy as I then thought, but our very lives. I turned upon you, forgetting everything but the gnawing doubts in my mind, and demanded to know your plans once you were on the throne. Were the ugly rumours true? Would you tear down all that Father had built? Would you use him like the others had? I was white with anger, but you remained very quiet, letting me circle around you, listening and not listening.

"Sister..." you said.

"I don't want any romantic words from you!" I cried. But I saw that flashing smile on your face, the one I'd seen years ago when you brought me a bird you'd caught in the marshes.

"Let me tell you something…" you began, but I strode across the room, carefully avoiding the sumptuous bed strewn with flowers and sprinkled with a dozen different scents.

"Don't come any nearer… upstart!" I cried, and you followed me with your hand held out, smiling still, making a game of my anger. Then I trembled, for something delicate was moving within me, something raw and untouched.

"I'm not going to destroy the king," you said. "I'm going to restore him. What do you think he and I have been talking about these last four years? Now… look in my eyes, Beloved of Aton, and tell me who I remind you of…"

I looked and my hand flew to my mouth in surprise. The same narrow eyes, the same features, only softer, saner than his. Why had I not seen if before?

"Now you know why I call you *sister.* Once he asked me whose blood flowed in my veins, and was it the blood of Amenhotep. And I said, *No,* feeling at that moment something touch me soft and sharp as a wish. *No,* I said… and I whispered, *Royal brother, yours!* but his back was turned. Look, my mother Sitamon was his sister, and he lay with her – I know this, for he told me – when he was a boy no older than I. He doesn't really know if I am his… but he's watched me all these years. He called me the Child of the Aton, he called me his Beloved. Today he called me *his son.*"

"Who else knows?" I asked, my voice so soft I could scarcely hear it.

"No one. He says it would mean my death to have it known."

Now I looked at you and whispered "*brother,*" and the word was not strange on my tongue; it was as though I had spoken it inwardly a thousand times. We stared at each other and saw nothing but the shadow of the king our father who had made us one. Your flesh was my flesh; your mouth, my mouth. The great wings of the royal hawk thrashed the air between us. You took my hand in yours and placed it over your hard sex as once many years before you gave me the white wild bird you caught, to hold, to feel its shape and pulse, that I might not fear it.

"I don't want to hurt you, sister..."

"It will only be the first moment."

Then we were sinking into the vast bed of linen and flowers, into a private garden, into the magical painted floor of the palace to lose ourselves among the birds and lotuses. And we were lost among the magic squares, we were children lost in the bushes of Meru Aton, we were man and woman lost in the great bed which had become the world.

And I murmured from the depths of the garden, "Come down, my brother, come down." And you came and roughly ripped the collar of beads and flowers from my throat and threw it across the room where it fell in a hundred pieces. We watched each other's faces and smiled; we were on the verge of laughter, triumphant silver laughter of children no more children. Our eyes never closed, not once, as the profound flowers pulled us down and down. And when our bodies came together it was heaven descending upon earth and creating night. My loins rose and called you in, and the pain was a moment felt and forgotten like the pain the glass grasshopper once gave your finger. My body obeyed some instinct it never knew it possessed. It swam, it danced. It arched up once, and again – and the movement surprised you and you gasped, and the gates of your loins opened. And as the sweet salt seed burst from your sex another instinct made me open my mouth wide with a cry or a laugh—

"O my brother, yes, *yes!*"

The next morning your soul, like a new alien body, throbbed within mine. And across the room was a sea of beads from my broken collar.

The day we left the Horizon the quays were crowded with vessels flying bright ribbons and streamers; hundreds of masts rose from the river and the shores were lined with silent citizens waving limp flowers and palm leaves. From the west gate of the palace a long line of porters and officials came to follow us down the flowered path to the river. It was the same path we had walked as children, but now we were the co-rulers of Keme. Would we ever walk down that path again?

The silence of the crowds on the shoreline filled me with fear and the faces of the officials were drawn and tense. Father waited for us, motionless beneath a red and blue canopy, clutching the royal emblems to his breast as though he feared someone would take them away if he held them less tightly. Then you and he faced each other for the last time, and your eyes searched one another's eyes for a reassurance neither could give. There was nothing to say. You wore the Blue Crown, the helmet of war, the crown he had worn in his youth.

And when I embraced him his body felt like some great shivering plant that the merest wind could destroy.

The great boats pulled away from the shore and formed a long procession in the river. But the silence on the banks was the silence of a funeral, and I felt we were sailing upstream towards the Valley of Death in a blaze of boats, and that we were already dead.

I looked back and saw that the red and blue canopy had become a purple slash in the distance. I imagined him under it, still clutching the royal emblems, his knuckles dead white from the strain, a small river of blood running down his wrist. I screamed with fear and ran into the cabin, and you came and hid your head in my breast and whispered, "I know, I feel it too. Time closing in on us, *myriads of years,* a string of endless suns hanging about our necks. We are the land. Last night I was strong, I dreamed I was Horus the Avenger, plucking out my eye to save my father. I whispered, *I come to thee, Father, arise for me. I gather thy bones, I make thee whole...* but today I am weak. I feel him there, downstream. I feel we will not see him again!"

"Say no more!" I cried, and held you to me. We clung to each other because we were more than ourselves; we were *him,* we were his body, his blood, and in our embrace we held him together, and in our separation he fell apart. And only when we loved was he made whole.

For most of the journey we stayed in the cabin. Neither of us wanted to look at the river.

Do you remember the incredible old hag who came in front of our procession in the city of Amon, who stood before our litter and refused to give way? She traced a circle in the sand with one naked hideous foot and mumbled something under her breath. One of the guards stepped forward to remove her, but on seeing her face he winced and moved away. She screeched like an owl and came up beside you and bent her head down to yours and whispered something in your ear. I never learned what she said, you would never tell me... but the power of her words could be seen in the sudden pallor which drained your face. You drew back, your mouth taut; your hand flew to the insignia of the god which hung from your collar. The hag laughed and disappeared into the crowd.

And our scribe Pawah identified her. "*That,*" he said, "was the Divine Consort of Amon in the days of Amenhotep. That bundle of rags was once the High Priestess of Opet!"

I trembled with cold. I had heard that her power had been great. That gruesome witch with the filthy breath had once lain with the god Amenhotep as the earthly wife of Amon, and had wielded as much influence as the High Priest himself. It was said that hers was the voice of the oracle which had first cursed our father when he was a child. Today she had cursed you. I begged you to tell me what she had said, but your lips tightened, and the chill in my bones sank deeper.

And when we entered the gates of the palace of Amenhotep you remarked that it looked like the dry bones of a desert bird picked clean by vultures. I could not bring myself to believe that I had been born within those walls. The peaks of the West rose up beyond them, and it was as though we had already entered the land of death.

In those horrible months at the old capital there was one thing which frightened me more than the chaos which surrounded us. I did not conceive. Your seed did not take root in me. The simplest peasant could lie with his woman once in the fields and she'd become fertile, but though we lay together a hundred times I was empty. Was that the curse the witch placed upon you? I wept into the hollow place between your shoulder and collarbone and cried that the gods were taking their revenge on our father by making us sterile. You tried to soothe me with silly jokes and puns (*remyet, romyet,* man was made from the tears of the Creator) – but even as you did your own body trembled and we made love in furious, frightened defiance of whatever perverse force choked the life in our loins. I took to wearing a knotted cord around my neck as a charm – the kind that peasants use – made of small cowrie shells which looked like the vulva of a woman.

Then one night I dreamed I saw you slain on the altar of the sun, and the next morning I feared for you and took Pawah with me and went into the temple of Ra-Horakhte. I found you as in the dream, fallen across the altar. The gates of heaven broke and the great vaults collapsed around me. The universe burst in my head and the body of Nut with its flesh of stars was soaked red with your blood. Your face was turned down, as though in the shame of your own death, and you were one with the sacrifices. The Blue Crown lay at your feet. I bent over you and called your name.

Pawah went into the dark recesses of the shrine and sought out a servant and asked, "*Who did it?*" And the fool answered with a smirk, "Ask not who is guilty, but who is *innocent* these days, O scribe of Ankheprure!" Then your gentle Pawah struck the man across the mouth.

And when we went to take you away, my brother, the altar of the sun burned with its offerings and you lay among the bloody flowers and the bread.

The same day word came of the death of our father. I do not remember anything about the weeks that followed. I think perhaps I became Isis and kept watch over your body for endless days.

By the time your body was ready for burial Tutankhamon was already on the throne and your belongings had been seized. There was only one place to bury you – the filthy hole where the desecrators had thrown the shrine of Tiy. I cringed to think that such a foul place would be your house of death, but there was nowhere else.

We gathered together all we could find— cast-off bits of things in the palace, discarded pieces of furniture made for others. I felt as though I was combing the world for those miserable trinkets which would accompany you on your journey. Then the meagre furnishings assumed gigantic proportions in my imagination. I listed in my mind again and again the articles which would surround you, as though the repetition of the list would somehow increase their number. Even now it soothes me to remember them:

—Four magical bricks bearing the name our father bore when he first took the throne. We feared to insert your name in place of his, lest they crumble to dust.

—Four alabaster jars made for me when I was a girl, to contain my vital organs when I died. They had my portrait on the lids, and the irises of the eyes were black jasper. I had glass cobras added to the brows, and my name ground away from the surface of the jars.

—One small trinket box containing an inner box full of broken, useless things – small vases and playing wands and pendants of ibises, and a little silver goose head…

—And one of the coffins Father had made for me in the City of the Horizon. (Remember the day you stood behind me watching the artists work upon it? You saw a name and it made you afraid; now I know it was your own name you saw.) It was a middle coffin in the set of three, and we changed it from that of a princess to that of a king. It was as though my own body was being reworked to accommodate your death. My golden hands holding *ankhs* became your hands clutching the royal emblems – a crook and a flail of blue glass beads on rods of bronze. The gold mask which was my face became your face; a blue beard was added, and a green and gold cobra on the brow. The words on the strips which were to have run down my body were changed from feminine to royal male, and down the length of the coffin from chest to foot the brilliant red and blue letters were adjusted to spell your name: *Beloved of the King of the Upper and Lower Land who lives in Truth, Lord of the Two Lands, the goodly child of the living Aton, who lives forever and ever. Smenkhare.*

It took the workers from twilight to dawn to drag the poor furnishings down the stairs into the shabby hole and arrange your house of death. We paid them well, but they never knew who they were burying. When first we led them through the dark Valley they were quiet, but when they saw where we were going they let up shrieks and groans and vowed they would approach no closer the dirty little tomb where the desecrators had thrown Tiy's shrine. A serpent dwelled within it, they said, with eyes that could paralyse a man and render him mad and impotent for the rest of his days.

Then with one great sweeping gesture Pawah lifted the sheet from your coffin and pointed to the royal cobra on the brow whose eyes gleamed in the moonlight. "There is yet another serpent whose gaze can paralyse a man!" he cried. And as they shrank back in fear he shouted, "Choose!" They chose, and continued their work.

But during the night it required more gold to hold them to their task, for one of them kept scaring his companions out of their wits by pointing to moving shadows on the tomb walls or claiming that the coffin lid had burst open of its own accord, or by stepping over the collapsed walls of Tiy's shrine with his feet making a noise like that of a barking dog against the thin metal. The night was filled with their prayers to Amon and Ptah and Hathor until they had called down the entire colony of the gods to protect them in their deed. Once one of the men, who was very drunk, fell down trembling and begged to be allowed to go home, but at that very moment the others accidentally banged the coffin against the shrine, and he took it as a sign of royal anger. Green-faced and gasping, he went about his work.

When it was over, I stood alone in the tomb, aware for the first time of the peeling plaster and the reeking dampness of the walls. An old leak near the door had been cemented over once in the past, but now it opened again, and a trickle of water crawled along the floor towards the lion-headed bier which supported your coffin. One drop per hour, maybe more, maybe less, would flow beneath your body. One drop per hour for eternity... enough to rot the bier, the coffin and all its contents! There was no time now to shift you to the eastern wall. How many years until those drops attack the wood of the bier, then soak through and soften the linen strips which bind you... and then seep into your flesh?

I put my fist to my mouth to stop the scream. I removed the white sheet from the coffin and in the half-light from the torches I saw something else. There was a thin line of shadow along the side where the lid had slipped open from rough handling. That child's coffin was too small for a man... and some of the gilt plating had been knocked off from the foot-end when it had lurched and bumped down the stairs of the shaft.

I heard an argument going on outside; the burial crew was threatening to return home without sealing up the tomb unless their payment was doubled. Pawah's angry words echoed down the shaft. "Scum! Drunkards and death mongers! You've been paid enough. Scavengers – you would turn around and break open this same tomb tomorrow if there was enough wealth in it. But I warn you, this place is doubly cursed!"

There was a silence and I heard Pawah lower his voice and invent a last cunning story to scare them off. "Do you know who you've buried this night?" he asked. And into the uncomprehending silence which followed he flung the words, "You've buried the bones of Tiy, who was a commoner like yourselves and whose body was destroyed on the pyres of the desecrators!"

They fell at the mouth of the tomb blubbering with horror. Not one of them would reveal the whereabouts of the place, not now.

I stood over you. All the torches had flickered out save one, and its light played upon your golden mask, your hands. I suddenly remembered that of the three coffins – past, present and future – this was the middle one, the present. Only it had survived, for the past was destroyed and the future unsown. Inside it you lay with one of my collars about your neck and three of my bracelets on each of your arms. Your fingers were capped with little caps of gold; once your living fingers upon me had been warm as the sun. And you were crowned, for days before I had torn the golden vulture from your chest and twisted it round and round and placed it on your head.

You lay in the attitude of a woman as we had arranged you – left arm across the chest, right arm straight down with the hand against the thigh, to mislead anyone who might one day find you and think you were the Beloved of the Criminal.

I knelt at your feet and read the prayer which was cut into the gold foil:

I breathe the sweet air from your mouth
And gaze upon your beauty every day.
To hear your voice like the north wind
Is all I pray,
For love will give life to my bones.

Give me the hands that hold your soul
And I will receive your soul and never die.
Call upon me by name forever and ever
And never shall it sound without reply.

Then I heard myself crying "*Smenkhare!*" the syllables bursting upon the foul air of the tomb, their sweetness for a moment erasing the salt smell of death. "*Smenkhare, Smenkhare!*"...

remembering the time when as children we had run laughing to the river-bank, our feet tangled in flowers and river-plants, the kiss in the bushes of Meru Aton, the drop of blood on your finger from the glass ornament. I had laughed then, to see your blood. And in my mind an old song:

O fair boy, come to your house,
I am your sister whom you love,
You cannot leave me
My brother, my brother!

... The bed of ebony and straw, our bodies straining the woven cord beneath us, my necklace of cowrie shells clattering and protesting in our dance of love...

"The dawn!" Pawah shouted from the top of the shaft.

I did not answer, for there was one thing left to do. Now I was unreal, yet fully real. It did not seem strange to me when I found myself hovering over you like Isis hovered over Osiris in the form of a hawk. Nor when I felt myself lying along you, the length of my body along the full length of the gold and turquoise and carnelian letters, the brilliant signs which spelled your name. Then the name was burned into my own flesh from breast to foot. My arms were the wings of death embracing you, and it seemed my loins received your last gift, the seed of your death.

Then I stepped over Tiy's shrine which still lay unhinged at the entrance. Banged up and beaten, it bore the titles of that fearful woman who was my grandmother. On the panel she and Father were making burnt offerings to the god; his image had been obliterated, yet the marks of its obliteration were deeper than the outlines of her body.

I went up the filthy stairs out of the tomb, and stepped out of the foul dampness of your eternal house and into the slanting rays of dawn. The workers re-sealed the tomb with the seal of the nine captives beneath the jackal, the symbol of the priestly college of Amon-Ra. The seal of the past had been broken only once, and then restored.

The rays of the Aton were remote, virginal. The power of the god was in its rawest form. Things were merely being *lit* by it, not drawn towards it. Was this the horror that my father had felt, was this his private fear – the *remoteness* of the god? There was nothing beneficial now in those awful rays, nor did it seem to me there was anything simple about dark and light – for this cold impersonal dawn was for me another kind of darkness, a new and secret form of night.

My life is worthless now as a grain of chaff or a single bead. But I don't fear death. You lie within my own coffin, and it is like the shell of my body containing you forever. You are caressed by my great wings of red and blue and gold. My end is upon me, but it is my victory. *Smenkhare!* I possess your secret name; did you not grant me your eternal soul when you told it to me? O my brother, your breath is locked forever in my ears where once the name was whispered, and I defy eternity to take from me what is mine!...I have just remembered something. Before I left your tomb I pulled a single cowries shell from my collar and placed it in the dirt at your feet. Your *ba* will see it glittering there forever like a small brilliant vulva, the entrance and the exit of life. You will remember the curled and swirling passages of our love. *You will call upon me by name and never*

HOUSE OF THE WHALE

Of course I was never a whale; I was an Eagle. This prison is a cage for the biggest bird of all. I'm waiting for them to work their justice, you see, and while I'm waiting I'm writing to you, Aaron, good friend, joker. The hours pass quickly here, strange to say; I have all kinds of diversions. The nice fat guard with the bulbous nose and the starfish wart at the tip often greets me as he makes his rounds. I make a point of waiting at the front of the cell when I know he's coming. And then there's Mario in the next cell who taps out fascinating rhythms at night with his fingernails against the walls.

I don't have an eraser with me, Aaron, so any mistakes I make will have to stay as they are, and when the pencil wears down, that will be that.

I can't help thinking how young I still am— 23. Twenty-three. Can I tell you about my life again? It was normal at first. I wrenched my mother's legs apart and tore out of her belly, trailing my sweet house of flesh behind me. I lay on a whaleskin blanket and watched the water; I sucked milk; I cried. I was wrapped up in thick bearskin in winter. I was bathed in the salt water of the sea. My mother was taller than all the mountains from where I lay.

There were the Ravens and the Eagles. You already know which I was. When I was old enough to take notice of things around me, I saw the half-mile line of our houses facing the waters of Hecate Strait. And I saw the severe line of the totems behind them, guarding the village, facing the sea – some of them vertical graves for the dead chiefs of old. Some totems, even then, had fallen, but our Eagle still looked down on us from the top of the highest one, presiding over the angular boats on the beach, the rotting cedar dugouts and black poplar skiffs. (Someone ages before had suggested getting motors for them – the boats, that is – and the old men of the village almost died.)

I was turned over to my uncle's care after I passed infancy, and he spoke to me in the Skittegan tongue and told me tales in the big cedar plank house. I've long since forgotten the language, you know that, but the stories remain with me, for stories are pictures, not words. I learned about the Raven, the Bear, the Salmon-Eater and the Volcano Woman – just as your children someday will learn all about Moses or Joshua or Christ.

I never knew my father; after planting me in my mother's belly he left to go and work in the Commercial Fisheries on the mainland. He forsook the wooden hooks and cuttlefish for the Canneries – who could blame him? Secretly, I admired him and all those who left the island to seek a fortune elsewhere, to hook Fate through the gills. But he never came back.

Our members had once been in the thousands, but had dwindled to hundreds. My grandfather, who was very old, remembered the smallpox that once stripped the islands almost clean. He remembered how the chiefs of the people were made to work in the white man's industries with the other men of the tribe, regardless of their rank; he remembered how the last symbols of authority were taken away from the chiefs and *shamans*. A chief once asked the leader of the white men if he might be taken to *their* island, England, to speak with the great white princess, Victoria – but he was refused.

Sometimes I heard my grandfather cursing under his breath the Canneries and hop fields and apple orchards on the mainland. I think he secretly wished that the Sacred-One-Standing-and-Moving, who reclined on a copper box supporting the pillar that held the world up, would shift his position and let the whole damn mess fall down.

When I was young some of our people still carved argillite to earn extra money. It was a dying art even then, but the little slate figures always brought something on the commercial market. The Slatechuk quarry up Slatechuk Creek wasn't far from the Skidegate; and there was an almost inexhaustible supply of the beautiful black stone, which got shaped into the countless figures of our myths. I remember having seen Louis Collison, the last of the great carvers, when I was still a child. I watched his steady gnarled hands creating figures and animals even I didn't know about, and I used to imagine that there was another Louis Collison, a little man, who lived inside the argillite and worked it from the inside out.

(The fine line, Aaron, between what is living and what is dead... what do I mean, exactly? That party you took me to once in that rich lady's house where everyone was admiring her latest artistic acquisition – a *genuine Haida* argillite sculture. It illustrated the myth of Rhpisunt, the woman who slept with a bear and later on bore cubs, and became the Bear Mother. Well, there were Rhpisunt and the bear screwing away in the black slate; Rhpisunt lay on her back, legs up, straddling the beast, her head thrown back and her jaws wide open with delight – and Mrs. What's-Her-Name kept babbling on and on about the 'symbolic' meaning of the carving until I got mad and butted in and told her it was obviously a bear screwing a woman, nothing more, nothing less. She looked upset, and I was a little drunk and couldn't resist adding, 'You see, I too am *genuine Haida*.' And as the party wore on I kept looking back at the elaborate mantelpiece and the cool little slate sculpture, and it was dead, Aaron, it had *died* – do you see?)

My mother wove baskets sometimes and each twist and knot in the straw was another year toward her death. And she sometimes lit the candlefish, the *oolakan* by night, and we sat around its light, the light of the sea, the light of its living flesh. Sometimes the old *shaman* would join us, with his dyed feathers and rattles, and do magic. I saw souls and spirits rising from his twisted pipe; I saw all he intended me to see, though most of the people left in the village laughed at him, secretly of course.

My grandfather was so well versed in our legends and myths that he was always the man sought out by the myth-hunters – museum researchers and writers from the mainland – to give the Haida version of such and such a tale. My last memory of him, in fact, is when he was leaning back in his chair and smoking his pipe ecstatically and telling the tale of Gunarh to the little portable tape recorder that whirred beside him. Every researcher went away believing he alone had the authentic version of such and such a myth, straight from the Haida's mouth – but what none of them ever knew was that grandfather altered the tales with each re-telling. 'It will give them something to fight about in their books,' he said. The older he got, the more he garbled the tales, shaking with wicked laughter in his big denim overalls when the little men with tape recorders and notebooks went away.

Does he think of me now, I wonder? Is he still alive, or is he lying in a little Skidegate grave after a good Christian burial – a picture of an eagle on the marble headstone as a last reminder of the totem of his people? Is he celebrating his last *potlache* before the gates of heaven, and has the *shaman* drummed his long dugout through waves of clouds? Are the ceremonial fires burning now, and is my grandfather throwing in his most precious possessions – his blue denim overalls, his pipe?

(Remember, Aaron, how amazed you were when I first told you about the *potlache*? 'Why didn't the chiefs just *exhibit* their wealth? you argued, and I told you they felt they could prove their wealth better by demonstrating how much of it they could *destroy*. Then you laughed, and said you thought the *potlache* had to be the most perfect parody of capitalism and consumer society you'd ever heard of. 'What happened,' you asked, 'if a chief squandered everything he owned and ended up a poor man?' And I explained how there were ways of getting wealthy again – for instance, the bankrupt chief could send some sort of gift to a rival chief, knowing that the returned favour had to be greater than the original one. It was always a matter of etiquette among our people to outdo another man's generosity.)

Anyway, I lie here and imagine grandfather celebrating a heavenly *potlache* – (heaven is the only place he'll ever celebrate it, for it's long since been forbidden by the government here on earth) – and the great Christian gates are opening for him now, and behind him the charred remains of his pipe and his blue denims bear witness to the last *potlache* of all.

Some of my childhood playmates were children of the white teacher and doctor of Skidegate, and I taught them how to play *Sin*, where you shuffle marked sticks under a mat and try to guess their positions. They got sunned up in summer until their skins were as copper as mine; we sat beneath the totems and compared our histories; we sat by the boats and argued about God. I read a lot; I think I must have read every book in the Mission School. By the time I was fifteen I'd been to the mainland twice and come back with blankets, potato money and booze for the old *shaman*.

I began to long for the mainland, to see Vancouver, the forests of Sitka spruce in the north, mountains, railroads, lumber camps where Tsimsyan and Niskae workers felled trees and smashed pulp. My uncle had nothing to say when I announced that I was going to go and work at 'the edge of the world' – but my grandfather put up a terrific fight, accusing me of wanting to desert my people for the white man's world, accusing my mother of having given birth to a feeble-spirited fool because on the day of my birth she accepted the white man's pain-killer and lay in 'the sleep like death' when I came from her loins. And then he went into a long rambling tale of a day the white doctor invited the *shaman* in to witness his magic, and the *shaman* saw how everything in the doctor's room was magic white, to ward off evil spirits from sick flesh, and he saw many knives and prongs shining like the backs of salmon and laid out in neat rows on a white sheet; from this he understood that the ceremony would not work unless the magical pattern of the instruments was perfect. Then the doctor put the sick man into the death-sleep, and the *shaman* meanwhile tried to slip the sick soul into his bone-box, but he couldn't because the doctor's magic was too powerful to be interfered with. It was only when the doctor laid out exactly four knives and four prongs onto another white sheet, that the *shaman* realized the doctor had stolen the sacred number four from us to work his magic.

I worked north in a lumber camp for a while; we were clearing a patch of forest for an airplane base. In one year I don't know how many trees I killed – too many, and I found myself whispering 'Sorry, tree' every time I felled another one. For *that* I should be in prison – wouldn't you think? Wasn't it worse to destroy all those trees than do what I did? Oh well, I can see you're laughing in your beer now, and I don't blame you. anyway, I really wanted to tell you about Jake and the other guys in the bunkhouse, and what a great bunch they were. I learned a lot about girls and things from them, and since I didn't have any stories of my own like that to tell them, I told them the myth of Gunarh – you know the one; you said the first part of it's a lot like a Greek myth – and all the guys gathered around, and Jake's mouth was hanging open by the time I got to the part about Gunarh's wife eating nothing but the sweetbreads of male seals...

'Then she took a lover,' I went on, 'and her husband discovered her infidelity and made a plan.'

'Yea, yea, go on, he made a *plan*!' gasped Jake.

'He—'

'SHADDUP, YOU GUYS, I'M TRYING TO LISTEN!'

'When they were asleep after a hard night, the lover and the wife...'

'Hear that, guys— a HARD night!'

'Jake, will ya SHADDUP!!'

'—Gunarh came in and discovered them together. He killed the lover and cut off his head and his – '

'Jesus CHRIST!'

'Jake, will ya SHADDUP!!'

'—and put them on the table...'

'Put *what* on the table?'

'It ain't the *head* boys!'

'Jesus CHRIST!'

'So the next morning his wife found her lover gone, and she went to the table for breakfast – you remember what she usually ate – and instead of...'

'O no! I'm sick, you guys, I'm sick!'

'SHADDUP!'

'—well, she ate *them* instead.'

'Jake, will ya lie down if you can't take it?'

I never did finish the story, because they went on and on all night about what Gunarh's wife ate for breakfast, and Jake kept waking up and swearing he was never going to listen to one of my stories again, because it was for sure all Indians had pretty dirty minds to think up things like that.

Almost before I knew it, my year was up and I was on a train heading for Vancouver; the raw gash I had made in the forest fell back behind me.

At first I spent a week in Vancouver watching the people carry the city back and forth in little paper bags; I stayed in a strange room with a shape like a big creamy whale in the cracked plaster on the ceiling, and curtains coloured a kind of boxcar red that hung limply and never moved. I drank a lot and had some women and spent more money than I intended, and after standing three mornings in a row in a line-up in the Unemployment Office, I bumped into you, Aaron, remember, and that was the beginning of our friendship. You had a funny way of looking at a person a little off-centre, so I was always shuffling to the left to place myself in your line of focus. I can't remember exactly what we first talked about; all I know is, within an hour we'd decided to hitch-hike to Toronto, and that was that. At first I hesitated, until you turned to me staring intently at my left ear and said, 'Lucas George, you don't want to go back to Skidegate, you're coming east.' And it was that careless insight of yours that threw me. You always knew me well, my friend. You knew a lot, in fact – and sometimes I was sure you kept about 50% of your brain hidden because it complicated your life. You were always a little ahead of yourself – was that the reason for your nervousness, your impatience? You could always tell me what I was thinking, too. You told me I was naïve and you liked me for that. You predicted horrible things for me, and you were right. You said my only destiny was to lose myself, to become neither Indian nor white but a kind of grey nothing, floating between two worlds. Your voice was always sad when you spoke like that...

Hey Aaron, do you still go through doors so quickly that no one remembers seeing you open them first?

My grandfather's tales, if he's still alive, are growing taller in Skidegate. My mother's baskets, if she's still alive, are getting more and more complicated – and the salmon are skinnier every season. My time's running out, and I'd better finish this letter fast.

You were silent in BC but you talked all the way through Alberta and Saskatchewan; we slept through Manitoba and woke up in Ontario. The shadows of the totems followed me, growing longer as the day of my life grew longer. The yellow miles we covered were nothing, and time was even less.

'Lucas,' you turned to me, 'I forgot to tell you something. In BC you were still something. Here, you won't even exist. You'll live on the sweet circumference of things, looking into the centre; you'll be less than a shadow or a ghost. Thought you'd like to know.'

'Thanks for nothing,' I said. 'Anyway, how do *you* know?'

'I live there too, on the circumference,' you said.

'What do you do, exactly?'

'I'm an intellectual bum,' you answered, 'I do manual work to keep my body alive. Sometimes I work above the city, sometimes I work below the city, depending on the weather. Skyscrapers, ditches, subways, you name it, I'm there…'

Aaron, I only have a minute left before they turn the lights out for the night. I wanted to ask you…

too late   out
      they're

'Well,' you said, the first day we were in the city, 'Welcome to the House of the Whale, Lucas George.'

'What do you mean?' I said.

'Didn't you tell me about Gunarh and how he went to the bottom of the sea to rescue his wife, who was in the House of the Whale.'

'Yes, but—'

'Well I'm telling you *this* is the House of the Whale, this city, this place. Ask me no questions, and I'll tell you no lies. This, this is where you'll find your *psyche*.'

'My *what*?'

'This is where you'll find what you're looking for.'

'But, Aaron, I'm not looking for anything really!'

'Oh yes you are…'

We stood looking at City Hall with its great curving mothering arms protecting a small concrete bubble between them. Behind us was Bay Street and I turned and let my eyes roll down the narrow canyon toward the lake. 'That's the Wall Street of Toronto,' you said. 'Street of Money, Street of Walls. Don't worry about it; you'll never work there.'

'So what's down there?' I asked, and you pointed a finger down the Street of Walls and said, 'That's where the whales live, Lucas George. You know all about them, the submerged giants, the supernatural ones…'

'The whales in our stories were gods,' I protested. And you laughed.

'I wish I could tell you that this city was just another myth, but it's not. It smacks too much of reality.'

'Well, *what else!*' I cried, exasperated with you. First it's a whale house, then you want it to be a myth – couldn't it just be a city, for heaven's sake?'

'Precisely. That's precisely what it is. Let's have coffee.'

We walked past City Hall and I asked you what the little concrete bubble was for.

'Why, that's the egg, the seed,' you said.

'Of *what*?'

'Why, Lucas George, I'm surprised at you! Of the *whale*, of course! Come on!'

'Looks like a clam shell to me,' I said. 'Did I ever explain to you where mankind came from, Aaron? A clam shell, half-open, with all the little faces peering out…'

'I'll buy that,' you said. 'It's a clam shell. Come on!'

I got a job in construction, working on the high beams of a bank that was going up downtown. 'Heights don't bother you Indians at all, do they?' the foreman asked me. 'No,' I said. 'We like tall things.'

He told me they needed some riveting work done on the top, and some guys that had gone up couldn't take it – it was too high even for them. So I went up, and the cold steel felt strange against my skin and I sensed long tremors in the giant skeleton of the bank, and it was as if the building was alive, shivering, with bones and sinews and tendons, with a life of its own. I didn't trust it, but I went up and up and there was wind all around me. The city seemed to fall away and the voices of the few men who accompanied me sounded strangely hollow and unreal in the high air. There were four of us – a tosser to heat the rivets and throw them to the catcher who caught them in a tin cup and lowered them with tongs into their holes – a riveter who forced them in with his gun, and a bucker to hold a metal plate over the hole. They told me their names as the elevator took us to the top – Joe, Charlie, Amodeo. I was the bucker.

Amodeo offered me a hand when we first stepped out onto a beam, but I couldn't accept it, although the first minute up there was awful. I watched how Amodeo moved; he was small and agile and treated the beams as if they were solid ground. His smile was swift and confident. I *did* take his hand later, but only to shake it after I had crossed the first beam. I kept telling myself that my people were the People of the Eagle, so I of all men should have no fear of walking where the eagles fly. Nevertheless when we ate lunch, the sandwich fell down into my stomach a long long way as if my stomach was still on the ground somewhere, and my throat was the elevator that had carried us up.

I found that holding the metal plate over the rivet holes gave me a kind of support and I was feeling confident and almost happy until the riveter came along and aimed his gun and WHIRR-TA-TA-TAT, WHIRR-TA-TA-TAT! My spine was jangling and every notch in it felt like a metal disc vibrating against another metal disc. After a while, though, I got the knack of applying all sorts of pressure to the plate to counteract some of the vibration. And when the first day was over I was awed to think I was still alive. The next day I imagined that the bank was a huge totem, or the strong man Aemaelk who holds the world up, and I started to like the work.

I didn't see you much those days for I was tired every night, but once I remember we sat over coffee in a restaurant and there was an odd shaky light in your eyes, and you looked sick. A man at a nearby table was gazing out onto the street, dipping a finger from time to time into his coffee and sucking it. I asked you why he was so sad. 'He's not a whale,' you answered.

'Then what is he?' I asked.

'He's a little salmon all the whales are going to eat,' you said. 'Like you, like me.'

'Where are you working now, Aaron?'

'In a sewer. You go up, Lucas, and I go down. It fits. Right now I'm a mole and you're the eagle.'

Aaron, I've got to finish this letter right now. I don't have time to write all I wanted to, because my trial's coming up and I already know how it's going to turn out. I didn't have time to say much about the three years I spent here, about losing the job, about wandering around the city without money, about drinking, about fooling around, about everything falling all around me like the totems falling, about getting into that argument in the tavern, and the fat man who called me a dirty Indian, about how I took him outside into a lane and beat him black and blue and seeing his blood coming out and suddenly he was dead. You know it all anyway, there's no point telling it again. Listen, Aaron, what I want to know now is:

Is my grandfather still telling lies to the history-hunters in Skidegate?

Are the moles and eagles and the whales coming out of the sewers and subways and buildings now that it's spring?

Have all the totems on my island fallen, or do some still stand?

Will they stick my head up high on a cedar tree like they did to Gunarh?

Will the Street of Walls fall down one day like the totems?

What did you say I would find in the House of the Whale, Aaron? Aaron? Aaron?

THE CARNIVAL

1

I danced before I learned to walk
And spoke before I learned to talk
I can do almost anything
But me myself I cannot sing.
Who am I, and who
Lives in the carnival behind my eye?

I swallow swords, I swallow fire
Twice a day for a very small fee
I am everyone's desire.
Do you know me?
I escape from ropes and chains
But I am not free, I am
The juggler juggling worlds behind your eye
I am the prisoner of me.

Who escapes from all the knots
The world can tie?
I swallow my words like swords
And cry
Who am I, and who
Lies in the carnival behind my eye?

2

I joined myself in the Mirror House
When all the children had gone home.
Hey! dancer, juggler, fire-eater, clown!
The crippled mirror stops you where you stand
The mirror has just stolen your left hand
And the whole glass house comes tumbling down.

I dance alone, I asked to dance alone
Inside the silver mirrors of my mind
Inside the living prison of my bones.

3

The wheel of the canival turns forever
and I am its crazy seasonal rider.
I can't get off it, either
For when I paid my fare I said:
I want a ticket for the endless ferris
Let me on it, let me on!
And the man said: *It'll cost you plenty,*
And I answered:
I can't stand to see the great wheel empty,
Let me on it, let me on!
And he said: *Okay, man, it's your money.*

But it's funny because sometimes
I'm glad I can't get off it.
I circle, I rise, I fall.
I seem to move better than anyone below
Even though I can't move at all.

4

I danced before I learned to walk
And spoke before I learned to talk
I can do almost anything
But me myself I cannot sing.
Who am I, and who
Lives in the carnival behind my eye?

The singer who falls back into the song
The dancer who falls back into the dance
Houdini who falls back into his chains
To imprison himself again,
To laugh.
Who lives in the carnival which is you?
I do, I do.

5

Ladies and gentlemen I'll dance for you
Twice a day for a very small fee
Or I'll break chains and swallow fire
If you follow me.
I'll juggle worlds before your eyes
I am the way, I am the light.
Lock me up and I'll be free
To dance forever, if you follow me.

FRAGMENTS FROM A CHILDHOOD

You are eleven years old and have finally decided you can fly. You've been through all the issues of the Marvel Family comics for the last three years, and you know the key word that will give you wings. You can fly if you pretend your white satin bed-jacket is a cape.

Now for you Shazam of the Creative Word, the Logos, the formula of flight. You know you can fly, the way They do, straight out like a bullet with your arms stretched forward and your cape fluttering in the wind.

There is no doubt in your mind.

Something else delays you.

You've tied the white satin bed-jacket around your neck tightly so that the wild sleepy folds fall down properly from the shoulders. You imagine what the wind will do to it; you know what it means.

You have many words to utter before you reach Shazam. You speak them slowly, half-hoping you will not reach the end of them, half-hoping that the world will not wring from you the Final Formula, for everything would stop then. You don't really want to pronounce the Unpronounceable.

You stand poised over the steep ravine that leads down to the river. You know it will work because it works for the Marvel Family. You think about the other kids who read the same comics but who don't know what they are all about. They *don't* know, otherwise they'd be here with you above the ravine with their bed-jackets tied around their necks, wouldn't they, wouldn't they? Maybe they do it alone in their rooms, maybe they pose alone in front of their mirrors, but none of them are here where you are now.

In a way you really do want to have the Great Word wrung out of you, but until now you've withheld it, having sworn never to pronounce it except in a moment of extremity. After all, you don't wish to destroy the world…

It's a long way down to the bottom of the ravine. There are no witnesses. You wanted it that way, didn't you?

Maybe God will punish you for your insolence. Icarus tried it once; Prometheus still lies chained to a rock with an eagle picking at his liver for a crime less than this. But the Marvel Family has no quarrel with God, and besides they do Good Works and have a fine sense of humour; God never punished them because they were Super.

Neither does Wonder Woman; she's a pagan and swears by obscure Greek deities. Anyway, you don't like her much because her costume is so American; Mary Marvel's costume is a hundred times better, although in the last issue her skirt was lengthened to below the knees and you were so mad you were going to write in to the editor about it.

You're still murmuring the introductory words; you realize you're coming to the end and in a minute you're going to have to say Shazam and take off into thin air above the ravine.

You know you can do it.

Something else delays you.

Well, the Marvel Family is so trite, for one thing. They just fly around, they never *discuss* anything. Are they aware of INFINITY for instance? Are they?

Do they know the Word is Ineffable, for instance?

Can any one of them even *spell* Ineffable?

You are trembling now and you say to yourself: Now I begin to suspect that my soul is greater than the soul of Mary Marvel. I've always known, deep down, that the Marvel Family are not very intelligent even though they fly and lightning shoots down and claims them.

Are they really interested in their marvels? Or do they just fly around, poor fools, casually tossing off the Word?

Can they eve SPELL the Word?

Holey Moley, all they can do is DO IT, for heaven's sake! But you, you can THINK about it, you know what it MEANS!

Suddenly you pity their lemon-yellow lightning bolts and their plastic boots. If Mary Marvel's skirt hadn't been lengthened, you might never have come to this moment of truth. You walk away in your white satin bed-jacket, sadder but wiser. It starts to rain and your miraculous cape drips all down your back.

Something has come to pass, you think, something more important than a mere flight over the ravine.

MYSTRAS

The Search for the Great White Horse

We streamed down the mountain from Tripoli in cold driving rain, on the trail of Constantine Palaeologus, last of the Byzantine emperors. We had heard (read?) (dreamed?) that his spirit still hovered over the city of Mystras, and that it had been known to appear in the guise of a great white horse on the deserted mountain stronghold. It seemed so important to us to discover the great lords, the dead ones – for they dwell in us still; their voices clamour in the night, they charge through our sleep like stallions.

So we went after the phantom beast, or the Emperor himself, whichever we would find.

To be as blindly specific as possible – we streamed down the mountain from Tripoli, and our cab driver who loved us more than life itself demonstrated the fact by taking the hairpin turns with a smiling nonchalance which chilled our blood. He informed us meanwhile that of all the people he had taken to Mystras, we were the first who wanted to go there to find a horse.

His name was George – *the* George, as they say in Greek, since all names in Greek are preceded by the definite article to make one feel like a being rather than a word – and we had discovered him in Naphlion drinking *gazoza* beside his cab stand and more than willing to take us to some of the more inaccessible parts of the Peloponnese.

Horrors of mist, sheer drops into raining nothingness awaited us at each bend in the mountain road. The mind gets used to such things, though the body curls up into a tight knot of terror and stays that way all down to the Acadian plain of sheep and goats and apples and tons of red, red earth. And from there even lower into Sparta, through narrow foggy valleys and passes, which, in the dark unreal rain, gave me a ghastly *déjà vu.*

You can't really begin to *think* in Greece until things get dark. It's the rain, or the dusk, or perhaps even a cloud or two which brings things into a reasonable perspective. All those tons of sunlight hammering away at the pillars of the Acropolis make history too lucid to be real, and you begin to wonder if light itself is a lie, a bright guise of God, not an illumination. Any maybe darkness is better, the darkness in which Constantine died, the dark end of the Byzantine Empire...

He was crowned on the 6th of January, 1449, in Mystras, provincial stronghold of the Empire, capital city of the Despotate of the Peloponnese. Then he went to Constantinople and died. In his life he defended what was left of the Empire, which was not much, for when he took the throne the Empire had to all intents and purposes fallen.

Through the Spartan plain, the rain still freezing, and ahead of us at last the abandoned phantom city.

'Panagea mou!' whispered the George. 'Isn't it beautiful!' and put his foot on the accelerator to bring us closer. The Greeks do not linger over beauty; they devour it.

Nikos said nothing and I merely murmured an ineffectual 'Wow,' for I had had a glimpse of Mystras and it seemed to me to be some incredible *thing*, beast or plant, all in fragments and clinging to the mountainside the way a nightmare clings to the mind of a sleeper. It was ghastly, green with rain, tragic with history, unspeakably *Byzantine!*

We had to pass through the modern village at the foot of the mountain. Here were the descendants of the people who had gradually abandoned the ancient stronghold to live in relative peace in the Spartan plain, having had their fill of Franks and Turks and who knows what else history had served them up both before and after Constantine. I was tempted to stop and ask one of them if they knew anything of the legend of the great white horse, but a shyness held me back. We slowed down, though, at a statue in the town square.

'Who's that?' the George asked one of the passersby, a small boy carrying a white goat on his shoulders.

'Oh *him*,' the boy smiled, 'that's Constantine.'

As we pulled away I tried to get a good look at the features of the statue, but I saw only an over-large metallic king with an amazingly determined face. He was dressed for war. I had expected him to be wearing a thin tubular Byzantine costume with little pointed slippers – like the ones you see on playing cards – but I suppose he only wore such things for religious ceremonies and public festivals. He had a beard, I think. And a helmet. I thought that since he had been crowned in January it would have been raining then too...

Most of the older men of the village were in the café – or *café-neon* as they say – drinking coffee or *ouzo* at that hour of the day, and as we passed through the narrow streets we heard their coaxing, argumentative voices, and the occasional clicking of the dice on the *tavali* boards.

The entrance to the phantom city was freezing stone. The trees wailed with cold, and I feared that the entire stronghold would somehow lose its grip on the mountainside and slide down into oblivion in a gush of mud and agony. But we paid our ten *drachmas* to the guard at the gate – a sullen fellow who was fortified on that particular day with a hefty bottle of *Metaxa* brandy – bought two guide-books which got immediately soaked, covered our heads with the latest newspapers from Athens, and passed out from under the arch.

Nikos uttered an exclamation of alarm. We had expected a ghost town, but this was ridiculous. It took us a while to comprehend what was confronting us – not a smallish wreck of a Byzantine stronghold, but an *entire city*, absolutely abandoned and broken. A city which wound up and up the mountainside in a steep maze which mocked our wildest dreams. The rain assaulted the cobblestones, the skeletons of mansions, the countless arches, the monasteries and chapels, the granaries, the palace of the Palaeologoi. And finally, on the very top, the castle which we had to bend over backwards to see. It dawned on me – (strange how the obvious dawns on you at times like these) – that they built castles on the tops of mountains so nobody could *reach* them.

In a limp attempt to bring things down to earth, I muttered 'Where's the George?' and imagined to my horror that our mad friend had driven up the highway to await us at the castle gate, the last exit of Mystras, the absolute top, from which, for some obscure reason, he figured we would triumphantly emerge.

Our guide-books had turned to soup in our hands, and we flung them away, enraged. I noticed on the pavement one half-readable page – a diagram, a map of Mystras of such complex character that it would require two weeks of intensive study to comprehend. Where *were* we? The place needed a month, a year, ten years to understand, and we had a couple of hours. In dark rain. Newspapers on our heads. Frozen to the bone. The latest news from Athens slowly dripping into my hair – who got out of jail, who got put in, reasons for same, ecstatic anticipations of the forthcoming visit of Spiro Agnew, and ads for Vim detergent.

We became depressed; the city overpowered us. We slid accidentally into the courtyard of a church, having lost all hope of ever finding the great white horse.

But then I saw him.

Nor the horse, but *him,* Constantine, dressed in a long red tubular robe with pointed slippers. I saw his crown, his face, everything. The rain was a million bullets on the mosaic floor. I saw the drinking-place for the horses, I saw his retinue entering the chapel with heavy soaked velvet clothes, I saw the gilded priests crowning the last of the Palaeologoi, at the close of an empire.

And the ghastly rain kept falling, falling, and the ikons in the chapel were purple with cold. A purple mountain rose up behind us and the last Lord of the Byzantines was falling, falling to his knees before the golden faces of the Virgin and the Child, accepting the crown of a hopeless empire upon his head.

I stood in the doorway of the chapel, gazing first into the cold sanctuary of Christ, and then out into the pounding courtyard where the emperor trod in his little golden slippers, where the hooves of his horses trod, and the heavy boots of his endless guards.

All this is history, but it was only much later that I learned that out of all the countless churches and chapels in Mystras, it was this one, Saint Demetrius, which had been chosen for the coronation. This is accident, or miracle. I merely record what I saw.

Back out, then, into the everlasting deluge, coldest day of our lives, cursing the George who had abandoned us for the impossible heights of Mystras, the summit, the last refuge in times of siege. Sliding through arched avenues, peering despondently into abandoned homes. On a green patch of field a monstrous jungle-plant clung to the earth dripping rain like sweat. Barbaric greenery, and beneath, in the grass and rocks, the hugest snails in the world, closed now in their armoured shells, little fortresses of horror threatening at any moment to open.

Soaked to the soul, still we searched for the great white horse, but all we could see through the insane rain was the little playing-card king slipping and sliding ahead of us, flanked by guards and aides, all of them like us cursing the cold and the cobblestones. Constantine (perhaps?) cursing his own coronation and the empire he had to uphold, a thing which had crumbled before he was even born.

We had only covered about one-hundredth of the city before we knew we would have to give up and go back to the main gate. The chill in our bones was the chill of history, the endless sieges of Mystras, assassinations, slaughters. I began to see children's eyes staring out from vaulted doorways, and black-robed women clutching ikons of the Virgin to their breasts, praying for the relief of the city. I imagined the aristocracy up on the higher, safer slopes, perhaps under the protection of the palace or the castle, while the poor got butchered in their flimsy homes or in the streets by invading armies. I kept seeing the rain of war falling, falling. History-like a great mud-slide; human beings, snails, donkeys, plants all clutching the mountainside for dear life.

Where the hell was the George? He could save us from these thoughts if only he'd realize that we would emerge from the main gate, and not the top. We tried to get help from the guard, who had sadly slipped more or less under his desk from the effects of the *Metaxa*, but who managed, nevertheless, to put through a call to the summit gate. Whoever was in charge up there, though, had seen neither a car nor a George and had no idea what we were talking about.

"George, you, you jest of God!' I cried – (when I get mad I am very literary) – and madly flailed the air with what was left of the newspaper from Athens until it dropped in a pulp to the ground.

The guard smiled at us and shrugged his shoulders and gradually slid away from view. Mystras was slowly beginning to slide down the mountain – or so it looked to our feverish eyes. I peered out through the gate, down to the Spartan plain, and tried to imagine the ancient warriors taking winter baths in the Eurotas river. The thought warmed me a little.

We decided to make a mad dash down to the little restaurant called *Marmora* at the foot of the mountain and wait for the George there. The place, as it turned out, was full of British tourists – an odd group which called themselves the Wings, or the Eagles, or something like that. The members all seemed to be well over sixty, and they were soaked to the skin. It seemed obvious that they had attempted to Do Mystras, and failed.

Their leader, who resembled James Mason, and who wore a little emblem of a Wing (or was it an Eagle?) on his blazer, was beamingly addressing the dazed group. 'I must say,' he began, 'The weather is rather bad, don't you think? But let's look on the bright side of things, shall we?'

One very old fellow who had fallen asleep with his arms on the table looked up in horror at this remark.

'What I *think* we should do is this. Or rather, one or the other of *these*. That is, in fact: A We can proceed to tackle Mystras *regardless*, thus keeping to our original plan which involves pushing on to the caves tomorrow. Or – and this is B – we can all go back and have tea in Sparta, and Do Mystras tomorrow, in which case we must forfeit the *caves* and push on later to Olympia. At any rate, I leave the question with you and trust you will come to a decision among yourselves.'

He left off speaking and sat down at his special table – (all tour leaders seem to have special tables, for some reason) – with an intriguing-looking German lady who seemed to be a leader too, except that she didn't have a group.

'Caves, caves!' cried the gentleman who kept falling asleep over the table, as the group plunged into a heated debate on the best course of action.

'I say, I think we're doing this all *wrong*,' murmured an octogenarian in a bowler hat.

Eventually the group decided on Tea in Sparta and the forfeiture of the caves. Wise choice, I thought, as I downed some brandy and proceeded to become very worried about the George. Might he have had an accident in the blinding rain? I dreamed up awful possibilities of what might have befallen him, realizing that, after all, he had been a great guy, a paragon of a cab driver, a gentleman and a friend.

At which point, precisely, the George came strolling into the restaurant, perfectly dry and crisp, not a hair of his head out of place, and asked us where we had been.

'George!' I cried with utter relief, flailing the air with my celery stick and making threatening jabs in his direction. 'What happened? Did you meet the great white horse?'

The next day the snails came out of their shells. We had spent the night in Sparta and returned to Mystras early in the morning. The rain had stopped, but the ground was still chill and damp; the sky was fraught with windblown clouds and patches of a frightening kind of blue. The first snail I saw was in the doorway of the mansion of Lascaris; the thing was sitting there, protruding more than halfway out of its shell, green and bilious, possibly the most hideous thing I'd ever seen. The same green as the ghastly jungle-plant with its tendrils clinging to the slope, the turgid green of too much rain and history.

Nikos and the George began collecting snails, for it turned out that there were hundreds of them, giant ones, naked and exposed in the wet grass. They carried them in handkerchiefs and the handkerchiefs squirmed. The floors of the Lascaris mansion almost crumbled as we walked on them, and there were great holes underfoot through which we saw the cellars. A black nun was coming down the mountain leading a donkey laden with baskets; we realized that there *were* a few human inhabitants in Mystras – in the monastery of the Pantanassa higher up on the slopes. She greeted us with a very soft *kali mera*, then lowered her eyes and went on her way. The smell of wild mustard and thyme was everywhere, turning the air yellow and green.

In the chapel of the Pantanassa there were frescoed figures of saints with their eyes hacked out. The expungement was the work of Turks who, with their Moslem fear of images, wished to rid the figures of their holy power. They didn't realize that the eyeless faces would become, in some strange way, even more powerful and compelling than ever.

As we were leaving the Pantanassa we saw, as an apparition, the octogenarian with the bowler hat hobbling down the road from the castle, clutching a cane and a guide-book. He must have somehow broken away from the Wings (or the Eagles) who were Doing Mystras from the bottom up, and decided to proceed from the summit down. Someone must have driven him up to the summit gate by the main road. His eyes were red and watery from trying to make a safe descent on the treacherously slippery cobblestones, and at the same time from trying to make sense of the cryptic map of Mystras which the guide-book offered.

He paused a moment with his cane uplifted, pointing in the general direction of the Pantanassa. Then he checked the map. "Ahhh-*ha!*' he said, with a deep sigh of satisfaction, and hobbled vaguely towards his goal. 'Nevertheless,' we heard him mutter as he turned a steep corner in the road. 'I somehow feel I've done this all *wrong*.'

How he had ever made it alone down from the castle is something we shall never know. We only got as high as the palace, from which point the castle stronghold could be seen perched on the dizzying summit far above us.

And still no sign of the great white horse.

At a bend in the road leading to the palace, I felt invisible archers watching us from behind the walls – and as it turned out, there was a narrow vertical slit in one part of the fortifications which must have served as a bowman's lookout. Anyone approaching the palace could have easily been picked off by the sentry who had full visual command of that part of the road. And we – the new invaders – might have been shot by an arrow of mist from the bow of some ghostly archer who'd held his post for five hundred years.

If ever the great white horse would appear, it must be *here*, I thought, as we entered the gates of the palace. Here on the windy heights in the skeleton of Constantine's royal house – a long lonely bunch of arches and walls without roofs. Here with the wild changing sky above, with crazy-horse clouds charging over the Spartan plain against a background of vivid blue. Here where the eternal snails, ugly predators, smirked in the slippery grass. Constantine may have eaten *escargots*, safe within the walls of his palace while outside the wars raged on and the bowmen shot everybody who came up the royal road and failed to give the password. I imagined him sitting at the hewn wood table in mid-winter with a great fire going, his plate heaped with dozens of the beastly things all done up in tomato sauce and onions, like the ones I had once in Athens, or perhaps stuffed with spices and butter. European style. The zing of arrows down below, and lower still the poor people praying in the chapel of Saint Demetrius or huddling in doorways in the rain.

But this is all wrong; Constantine wasn't sitting and eating within the palace walls in wartime. He was out fighting the invaders – the invaders who wear the same faces, always, regardless of who they are.

The George was tired of carrying his handkerchief of snails around, so he dropped the whole thing onto the ground and left the beasts to fend for themselves. We lost him again as he went behind the palace to hunt for herbs or something. When he emerged, immaculate as ever, we made our way back down the maze of roads, and he spoke for the first time in hours. 'History is wonderful! *Panagea mou,* history is really wonderful! Imagine – they all lived here, and worked and ate and died, just as we live and work and eat and die. They were *like us.* It breaks the mind just thinking of it!'

We stopped then, realizing we had taken a wrong turn somewhere in the maze and had 'done the whole thing all wrong'; we had to wind our way back to what looked like a main road, which took a full ten minutes, because we had somehow gotten over to the other side of the mountain.

Panagea mou, I thought (which translates as 'my all-holy one,' meaning the Blessed Virgin Mary. Some Greeks pepper their speech with this epithet, as we do ours with 'Oh God,' to express the whole range of emotions.) Where is the great white horse, and why hasn't he appeared to us pilgrims who have come so far to find him?

'George,' I asked, 'what do you think about the great white horse?'

'The villagers will know,' he said.

'Will the guard at the gate know?' I asked.

'The guard at the gate knows nothing,' said the George with venom. 'He is a fool, one of the great mistakes of God, a fool and a fiend. We won't ask him.'

I made no comment. The streets had dried out by now and the stone had been restored to its original colours – pink and beige. Someone had flung an empty pack of Players into the courtyard of Saint Demetrius and my eyes went red with indignation. I remembered a poignant comment a little girl I knew had made about the basic difference between her life in Canada and her life in Greece. 'In Canada I used to get mad,' she said. 'But here – I get *really* mad!'

'We forgot to see the Aphendiko,' I said, stopping in my tracks and remembering an excerpt from the guide-book. 'The place where they have the pictures of the miracles of Christ. The Good Samaritan, the Wedding at Cana, the Healing of the Man With Dropsy, the Healing of the Blind Man, and tthe Healing of Peter's Mother-In-Law.'

'Nobody could heal Peter's mother-in-law,' said the George grimly. 'I know.'

As we left through the main gate, he flung the guard a foul look. I learned later that the previous day's episode in the rain had left them with an enduring hatred for one another. The George swore in the name of everything holy that he had left a message with the fellow to inform us of where he would be waiting. The guard, on the other hand, swore in the name of everything holy that he knew nothing of it.

We got into the freezing cab and made our way down to the serene village of Mystras at the foot of the mountain. As we turned a bend in the road, I looked back once and saw the crazy city clinging to the slopes. There was a small grey-white donkey in the distance.

"Ha!' I cried, becoming literary again. 'Another wild jest of God! We search for the great white horse and all we get is a donkey. I ask you!'

I fell back into the seat and lit a cigarette, sadder than I'd been for a long time, because Mystra was a miracle, and they're hard to come by these days, and I knew I might never go back, horse or no horse.

It was late afternoon in the village; no one was out of doors except a very slight old fellow who had just emerged from the *café-neon.*

'Hello – you there!' cried the George, rolling down the window and beckoning for the man to come over. 'We've come a long way to Mystras and we have heard of a legend of a great white horse – the ghost of the emperor Constantine.'

'Yes, we have heard that his spirit still hovers over the city and has been know to appear in that form,' I said. 'Please tell us – do you know of such a legend?'

The old fellow leaned in the window and shook his head slowly. 'I've lived here all my life,' he said wearily. 'And I don't know what you're talking about.'

'Please don't go!' I cried. 'Maybe it's a secret, maybe you don't like talking about it. But you can tell us! *Was* Constantine ever seen on the mountainside in the shape of a great white horse? Is it true, is it?'

The man gave a dry cough, excused himself, and turned away. We heard him mutter a moment later: 'You *xeni!* You outsiders – you think of everything...'

TROJAN WOMEN

1981

HELEN

A POEM BY YANNIS RITSOS

A TRANSLATION BY
GWENDOLYN MACEWEN
AND NIKOS TSINGOS

(Even from a distance the wear and tear showed – crumbling walls with fallen plaster; faded window-shutters; the balcony railings rusted. A curtain stirring outside the window on the upper floor, yellowed, frayed at the bottom. When he approached – hesitantly – he found the same sense of desolation in the garden: disorderly plants, voluptuous leaves, unpruned trees; the odd flower choked in the nettles; the waterless fountains, mouldy; lichen on the beautiful statues. An immobile lizard between the breasts of a young Aphrodite, basking in the last rays of the setting sun. How many years had passed! He was so young then – twenty-two? twenty-three? And she? You could never tell – she radiated so much light, it blinded you; it pierced you through – you couldn't tell anymore what she was, if she was, if you were. He rang the doorbell. Standing in the place he once knew so well, now so strangely changed with its unknown entanglement of dark colours, he heard the sound of the bell ringing, solitary. They were slow to answer the door. Someone peered out from the upper window. It wasn't her. A servant, very young. Apparently laughing. She left the window. Still no answer at the door. Afterwards footsteps were heard inside on the stairway. Someone unlocked the door. He went up. A smell of dust, rotten fruit, dried-up slop, urine. Over here. Bedroom. Wardrobe. Metal mirror. Two tottering carved armchairs. A small cheap tin table with coffee cups and cigarette butts. And she? No, no, impossible? An old, old woman – one, two hundred years old! But five years ago – Oh no! The bedsheet full of holes. There, unstirring; sitting on the bed; bent over. Only her eyes – larger than ever, autocratic, penetrating, vacant.)

Yes, yes— it's me. Sit down for a while. Nobody comes around
anymore. I'm starting.
to forget how to use words. Anyway, words don't matter. I think
summer's coming,
the curtains are stirring differently— they're— trying to say something—
such stupidities! One of them
has already flown out of the window, straining to break the rings,
to fly over the trees— maybe as well to haul
the whole house away— but the house resists with all corners
and me along with it, despite the fact that I've felt for months,
liberated
from my dead ones, my own self, and this resistance of mine,
incomprehensible, beyond my will, strange to me, is all I possess—
my wedlock
with this bed, this curtain— is also my fear, as though
my whole body were sustained by the ring with the black stone I
wear on my forefinger

Now, I examine this stone very closely now in these endless hours
of night—
it's black, it has no reflections— it grows, it grows, it fills up
with black waters— the waters overflow, swell; I sink,
not to the bottom, but to an upper depth; from up there
I can make out my room down below, myself, the wardrobe, the servants
quibbling voicelessly; I see one of them perched
on a stool and with a hard, spiteful expression,
polishing the photograph of Leda; I see the duster leaving behind
a trail of dust and delicate bubbles which rise and burst
with quiet murmuring all around my ankle-bones or knees.

I notice you also have a perplexed, dumbfounded face, distorted
by the slow undulations of black water— now widening, now
lengthening your face
with yellow streaks. Your hair's writhing upwards
like an upside down Medusa. But then I say: it's only a stone,
a small precious stone. All the blackness contracts, then
dries up and localizes in the smallest possible knot— I feel it
here, just under my throat. And I'm back again
in my room, on my bed, beside my familiar phials
which stare at me, one by one, nodding— only they can help me
for insomnia, fear, memories, forgetfulness, asthma.
What are you up to? Still in the army? Be careful. Don't
distress yourself so much
about heroism, honors and glories. What'll you do with them?
Do you still have
that shield on which you had my face engraved? You were so funny
in your tall helmet with its long tail— so very young,
and shy, as though you'd concealed your handsome face
between the hind legs of a horse whose tail hung all the way down
your bare back. Don't get mad again. Stay awhile longer.

The time of antagonism is over now; desires have dried up;
perhaps now, together, we can observe the same point of futility—
where, I think, the only true encounters are realized— however
indifferent,
but nonetheless soothing— our new community, bleak, quiet, empty,
without much displacement or opposition— let's just stir the ashes
of the fireplace,
making now and again long thin lovely burial urns
or sit down on the ground and beat it with soundless palms.

Little by little things lost their meaning, became empty; did
they ever perhaps mean anything?— slack, hollow;
we stuffed them with straw and chaff, to give them form,
let them thicken, solidify, stand firmly— the tables, chairs,
the bed we lay on, the words; always hollow
like the cloth sacks, the vendors' burlap bags;
from the outside you can already make out what's inside them,
potatoes, onions, wheat, corn, almonds, or flour.

Sometimes one of them catches on a nail on the stair
or on the prong of an anchor down in the harbour, it rips open,
the flour spills out— a foolish river. The bag empties itself.
The poor gather up the flour in handfuls to make
some pies or gruel. The bag collapses. Someone
picks it up from its two bottom ends; shakes it out in the air;
a cloud of white dust enfolds him; his hair turns white;
especially his eyebrows turn white. The others watch him.
They don't understand a thing; they wait for him to open his mouth,
    to say something.
He doesn't. He folds up the bag into four sections; he leaves
as he is, white, inexplicable, wordless, as though disguised
as a lewd naked man covered with a sheet,
or like a cunning dead man resurrected in his shroud.

So, events and things don't have any meaning— the same goes for
    words, although
with words we name, more or less, those things we lack, or which
we've never seen— airy, as we say, eternal things—
innocent words, misleading, consoling, equivocal, always

trying to be correct— what a terrible thing,
to have named a shadow, invoking it at night in bed
with the sheet pulled up to your neck, and hearing it, we fools
think
that we're holding our bodies together, that they're holding us,
that we're keeping our hold on the world.

Nowadays I forget the names I knew best or get them all mixed up—
Paris, Menelaus, Achilles, Proteus, Theoklymenos, Tefkros,
Castor and Polydeuces— my moralizing brothers; who, I gather
have turned into stars— so they say— pilot-lights for ships—
Theseus, Pireitheus,
Andromache, Cassandra, Agamemnon— sounds, only formless sounds,
their images unwritten on a window-pane
or a metal mirror or on the shallows of a beach, like that time
on a quiet sunny day, with myriads of masts, after the battle
had abated, and the creaking of the wet ropes on the pulleys
hauled the world up high, like the knot of a sob arrested
in a crystalline throat— you could see it sparkling, trembling
without becoming a scream, and suddenly the entire landscape, the
ships,
the sailors and the chariots, were sinking into light and anonymity.

Now, another deeper, darker submersion— out of which
some sounds emerge now and then— when hammers were pounding
wood
and nailing together a new trireme in a small shipyard; when a huge
four-horse chariot was passing by on the stone road, adding to
the ticks
from the cathedral clock in another duration, as though

there were more, much more than twelve hours and the horses
were turning around in the clock until they were exhausted; or when
    one night
two handsome young men were singing below my windows
a song for me, without words— one of them one-eyed; the other
wearing a huge buckle on his belt— gleaming in the moonlight.

Words don't come to me on their own now— I search them out as
    though I'm translating
from a language I don't know— nevertheless, I do translate.
    Between the words,
and within them, are deep holes; I peer through them as though
I'm peering through the knots which have fallen from the boards
    of a door
completely closed up, nailed here for ages. I don't see a thing.

No more words or names; I can only single out some sounds— a
    silver candlestick
or a crystal vase rings by itself and all of a sudden stops,
pretending it knows nothing, that it didn't ring, that nobody
struck it, or passed by it. A dress
collapses softly from the chair onto the floor, diverting
attention from the previous sound to the simplicity of nothing.
    However
the idea of a silent conspiracy, although diffused in air,
floats densely higher up, almost *immeasurable,*
so that you feel the etching of the lines around your mouth grow
    deeper
precisely because of this presence of an intruder who takes over
    your position

turning you into an intruder, right here on your own bed, in your
own room.

Oh, to be alienated in our very clothes which get old,
in our own skin which gets wrinkled; while our fingers
can no longer grip or even wrap around our bodies
the blanket which rises by itself, disperses, disappears, leaving
us
bare before the void. Then, the guitar hanging on the wall
with its rusty strings, forgotten for years, begins to quiver
like the jaw of an old woman quivering from cold or fear, and
you have to put your palm flat upon the strings to stop
the contagious chill. But you can't find your hand, you don't
have one;
and you hear in your guts that it's your own jaw that's shaking.

In this house the air's become heavy and inexplicable, maybe
due to the natural presence of the dead. A trunk opens
on its own, old dresses fall out, rustle, stand up straight
and quietly stroll around; two gold tassels remain on the carpet;
a curtain
opens— revealing nobody— but they're still there; a cigarette
burns on and off in the ashtray; the person who
left it there is in the other room, rather awkward,
his back turned, gazing at the wall, possibly at a spider
or a damp stain, facing the wall, so the dark
hollow under his protruding cheekbones won't show.

The dead feel no pain for us any more— that's odd, isn't it?—
not so much for them as for us— that neutral intimacy of theirs
within a place which has rejected them and where they don't
contribute
a thing to the upkeep, nor concern themselves with the run-down
condition,
them, accomplished and unchangeable, and yet seeming somewhat larger.

This is what sometimes confounds us— the augmentation of the
unchangeable
and their silent self-sufficiency— not at all haughty; they don't
try
to force you to remember them, to be pleasing. The women
let their bellies slacken; their stockings sagging, they take
the pins from the silver box; they stick them in the sofa's velvet
one by one, in two straight rows; then pick them up
and begin again with the same polite attention. Someone who's
very tall
emerges from the hall— he knocks his head against the door;
he doesn't make a single grimace— and neither could the knock be
heard at all.

Yes, they're as foolish as we; only quieter. Another of them
raises his arm ceremoniously, as though to give a blessing to
someone,
pulls off a piece of the crystal from the chandelier, puts it in his
mouth
simply, like glass fruit— you think he's going to chew it, to get
a human function

in motion again— but no; he clenches it between his teeth, thus,
to let the crystal shine with a futile brightness. A woman
takes some face-cream from the little round white jar
with a skilled movement of two of her fingers, and writes
two thick capital letters on the windowpane— they look like L and D—
the sun heats the glass pane, the cream melts, drips down the wall—
and all this means nothing— just two greasy, brief furrows.

I don't know why the dead stay around here without anyone's sympathy;
I don't know what they want
wandering around the rooms in their best clothes, their best shoes
polished, immaculate, yet noiselessly as though they never touch
the floor.
They take up space, sprawl wherever they like, in the two rocking
chairs,
down on the floor, or in the bathroom; they forget and leave the tap
dripping;
forget the perfumed bars of soap melting in the water. The servants
passing among them, sweeping with the big broom,
don't notice them. Only sometimes, the laughter of a maid
somewhat confined— it doesn't fly up, out of the window,
it's like a bird tied by the leg with a string, which someone is
pulling downward.

Then the servants get inexplicably furious with me, they throw the
broom
here, right into the middle of my room, and go into the kitchen;
I hear them
making coffee in big briquets, spilling the sugar on the floor—
it crunches under their shoes; the aroma of the coffee

drifts through the hallway, floods the house, observes itself
in the mirror like a silly, dark, impudent face covered with uncombed
    tufts of hair
and two false skyblue earrings, blows its breath on the mirror,
clouds the glass. I feel my tongue probing around in my mouth;
I feel that I've still got some saliva. 'A coffee for me too'—
    I call to the servants;
'a coffee,' (that's all I ask for; I don't want anything else).
    They
act as though they don't hear. I call over and over again
without bitterness or rage. They don't answer. I hear them
gulping down their coffee from my porcelain cups with the gold brims
and the delicate violet flowers. I become silent and gaze at
that broom flung on the floor like the rigid corpse
of that tall, slim young grocer's boy, who, years ago,
showed me his big phallus between the railings of the garden gate.

Oh yes, I laugh sometimes, and I hear my hoarse laughter rise up,
no longer from the chest, but much deeper, from the feet; even
    deeper,
from the earth. I laugh. How pointless it all was,
how purposeless, ephemeral and insubstantial— riches, wars, glories,
jealousies, jewels, my own beauty.
                                What foolish legends,
swans and Troys and loves and brave deeds.
                                I met my old
lovers again in mournful night feasts, with white beards,
with white hair, with bulging bellies, as though they were
already pregnant with their death, devouring with a strange craving
the roasted goats, without looking into a shoulder-blade— what
    should they look for?—

a level shadow filled all of it with a few white specks.
I, as you know, preserved my former beauty
as if by miracle (but also with tints, herbs and salves,
lemon juice and cucumber water). I was only terrified to see
  in their faces
the passing also of my own years. At that time I was tightening
  my belly muscles,
I was tightening my cheeks with a false smile, as though
propping up two crumbling wall with a thin beam.

That's how I was, shut in, confined, strained— God, what exhaustion—
confined every moment (even in my sleep) as though I were inside
freezing armor or a wooden corset around my whole body, or within
my own Trojan Horse, deceptive and narrow, knowing even then
the pointlessness of deceit and self-deception, the pointlessness of
  fame,
the pointlessness and temporality of every victory.
      A few months ago,
when I lost my husband (was it months or years?), I left
my Trojan Horse forever down in the stable, with his old horses,
so the scorpions and spiders could circle around inside him. I
  don't tint my hair anymore.

Huge warts have sprouted on my face. Thick hairs have grown
  around my mouth—
I clutch them; I don't look at myself in the mirror—
long, wild hairs— as though someone else has enthroned himself
  within me,
an impudent, malevolent man, and it's his beard

that emerges from my skin. I leave him be— what can I do?—
I'm afraid that if I chased him away, he'd drag me along behind him.

Don't go away. Stay awhile longer. I haven't talked for ages.
Nobody comes to see me anymore. They were all in a hurry to leave,
I saw it in their eyes— all in a hurry for me to die. Time doesn't
    roll on.
The servants loathe me. I hear them opening my drawers at night,
taking the lacy things, the jewels, the gold coins; who can tell
if they'll leave me with a single decent dress for some necessary
    hour
or a single pair of shoes. They even took my keys
from under my pillow; I didn't stir at all; I pretended I was
    asleep—
they would have taken them one day anyway— I don't want them to know,
    at least, that I know.

What would I do without even them? 'Patience, patience,' I tell
    myself;
'patience'— and this too is the smallest form of victory,
when they read the old letters of my admirers
or the poems great poets dedicated to me; they read them
with idiotic bombast and many mistakes in pronunciation,
    accentuation, metre
and syllabification— I don't correct them. I pretend I don't hear.
    Occasionally
they draw big moustaches with my black eyebrow pencil
on my statues, or stick an ancient helmet or a chamber-pot
on their heads, I regard them coolly. They get angry.

One day, when I felt a little better, I asked them again
to make up my face. They did. I asked for a mirror.
They had painted my face green, with a black mouth. 'Thank you,'
    I told them,
as though I hadn't seen anything strange. They were laughing. One
    of them
stripped right in front of me, put on my gold veils, and like that,
bare-legged with her thick legs began to dance,
leapt upon the table— frenzied; danced and danced, bowing
in imitation, as it were, of my old gestures. High up on her thigh
she had a love-bite from a man's strong even teeth.
I watched them as though I were in the theatre— with no humiliation
    or grief,
or indignation— for what purpose?— But I kept telling myself:
'one day we'll die,' or rather: 'one day you will,' and that
was a sure revenge, fear and consolation. I looked
everything straight in the eye with an indescribable, apathetic
    clarity, as if
my eyes were independent of me; I looked at my own eyes
situated a metre away from my face, like the panes
of a window far removed, from behind which someone else
sits and observes the goings-on in an unknown street
with closed coffee, photograph and perfume shops,
and I had the feeling that a beautiful crystal phial
broke, and the perfume spilled out in the dusty showcase. Everyone
    passing,
pausing vaguely, sniffing the air, remembered something good
and then disappeared behind the pepper-trees or at the end of the
    street.

Now and again, I can still sense that aroma— I mean, I remember it;
isn't it strange?— those things we usually consider great, dissolve,
fade away—
Agamemnon's murder, the slaughter of Clytemnestra (they'd sent me
one of her beautiful necklaces from Mycenae, made
from small gold masks, held together by links
from the upper tips of their ears— I never wore it). They're
forgotten;
some other things remain, unimportant, meaningless things; I
recall seeing one day
a bird perching on a horse's back; and that baffling thing
seemed to explain (especially for me) a certain beautiful mystery.

I still remember, as a child, on the banks of the Eurotas, beside
the burning leanders,
the sound of a tree peeling off alone; the bark
falling gently into the water and floating away like triremes,
and I waited, stubbornly, for a black butterfly with orange stripes
to land on a piece of bark, amazed that although it was immobile,
it moved,
and this broke me up, that butterflies, although adept in air,
know nothing about traveling in water, or rowing. And it came.

There are certain strange, isolated moments, almost funny. A man
takes a stroll at midday wearing a huge hamper on his head; the
basket
hides his whole face as though he were headless or disguised
by an enormous eyeless, multi-eyed head. Another man,

strolling along, musing in the dusk, stumbles over something,
curses,
turns back, searches— finds a pebble, picks it up; kisses it; then
remembers to look around; goes off guiltily. A woman
slips her hand inside her pocket; finds nothing; takes her hand
out,
raises it and carefully scrutinizes it, as though it were breathed
on by the powder of emptiness.

A waiter's caught a fly in his hand— he doesn't crush it;
a customer calls him; he's absorbed; he loosens his fist; the fly
escapes and lands on the glass. A piece of paper rolls down the
street
hesitantly, spasmodically, attracting nobody's
attention— enjoying it all. But yet, every so often
it gives off a certain crackle which belies it; as though looking for
an impartial witness to its humble, secret route. And all these things
have a desolate and inexplicable beauty, and a profound pain
because of our own odd and unknown gestures— don't they?

The rest is lost as though it were nothing. Argos, Athens, Sparta,
Corinth, Thebes, Sikion— shadows of names. I utter them; they
re-echo as though they're sinking
into the incomplete. A well-bred, lost dog stands
in front of the window of a cheap dairy. A young girl passing by
looks at it;
it doesn't respond; its shadow spreads wide in the sidewalk.
I never learned the reason. I doubt it even exists. There's
only
this humiliating compulsive (by whom?) approval

as we nod 'yes,' as though greeting someone
with incredible servility, though nobody's passing, nobody's there.

I think another person, with a totally colorless voice related to me
    one evening
the details of my life; I was sleepy and wishing deep inside
that he'd finally stop; that I could close my eyes,
and sleep. And as he spoke, in order to do something, to fight
    off sleep,
I counted the tassels on my shawl, one by one, to the tune of
a silly children's song of Blindman's Buff, until
the meaning got lost in the repetition. But the sound remains—
noises, thuds, scrapings— the drone of silence, a discordant weeping,
someone scratches the wall with his fingernails, a scissor falls
    onto the floor boards,
someone coughs— his hand over his mouth, so as not to awaken the
    other
sleeping with him— maybe his death— stops; and once again
that spiraling drone from an empty, shut-up well.

At night I hear the servants moving my big pieces of furniture;
they take them down the stairs— a mirror, held like a stretcher,
reveals the worn-out plaster designs on the ceiling; a windowpane
knocks against the railings— it doesn't break; the old overcoat on
    the coat-rack
raises its empty arms for a moment, slips them back into the pockets;
the little wheels of the sofa's legs creak on the floor. I can feel
right here on my elbow the scratching on the wall made by the corners
    of the wardrobe
or the big carved table. What are they going to do with them?

'Goodbye,' I say
almost mechanically, as though bidding farewell to a visitor who's
always a stranger. There's only
that vague droning which lingers in the hallway as though from the
horn
of downfallen hunting lords in the last drops of rain, in a burnt-out-
forest.
Honestly, so many useless things collected with so much greed
blocked the space— we couldn't move; our knees
knocked against wooden, stony, metallic knees. Oh, we've really
got to grow old, very old, to become just, to reach that
mild impartiality, that sweet lack of interest in comparisons,
judgments,
when it's no longer our lot to take part in anything except this
quietness.

Oh yes, how many silly battles, heroic deeds, ambitions, arrogance,
sacrifices and defeats, defeats, and still more battles for things
that others determined when we weren't there. Innocent people
poking hairpins into their eyes, banging their heads
on the high wall, knowing full well that it wouldn't fall
or even crack, just to see at least from a little crevice
a slight sky-blue unshadowed by time and their own shadows. Meanwhile—
who knows—
perhaps there, where someone is resisting, hopelessly, perhaps there
human history begins, so to speak, and man's beauty
among rusty bits of iron and the bones of bulls and horses,
among ancient tripods where some laurel still burns
and the smoke rises curling in the sunset like a golden fleece.

Stay awhile longer. Evening's falling. The gold fleece we spoke
of— Oh, thought
comes slowly to us women— it relaxes somehow. On the other hand
men
never stop to think— maybe they're afraid; maybe they don't want
to look their fear straight in the eye, to see their fatigue, to
relax—
timid, conceited, busybodies, they surge into darkness. Their
clothes
always smell of smoke from a conflagration they've passed by or
through
unwittingly. Quickly they undress; fling
their clothes onto the floor; fall into bed. But even their bodies
reek of smoke— it numbs them. I used to find, when they were finally
asleep,
some fine burnt leaves among the hairs on their chests
or some ash-grey down from slain birds. Then
I'd gather them up and keep them in a small box— the only signs
of a secret communion— I never showed these to them— they wouldn't
have recognized them.

Sometimes, oh yes, they were beautiful— naked as they were, surrendered
to sleep,
thoroughly unresisting, loosened up, their big strong bodies,
damp and softened, like roaring rivers surging down
from high mountains into a quiet plain, or like abandoned children.
At such times
I really loved them, as though I'd given birth to them. I noticed
their long eyelashes
and I wanted to draw them back into me, to protect them, or in
this way

to couple with their whole bodies. They were sleeping. And sleep
demands respect
from you, because it's so rare. That's all over too. All forgotten.

Not that I don't remember anymore— I do; it's just that the memories
are no longer emotional— they can't move us— they're impersonal,
placid,
clear right into their most bloody corners. Only one of them
still retains some air around it, and breathes.

That late afternoon,
when I was surrounded by the endless shrieks of the wounded,
the mumbled curses of the old men and their wonder of me, amid
the smell of overall death, which, from time to time glittered
on a shield or the tip of a spear or the metope
of a neglected temple or the wheel of a chariot— I went up alone
onto the high walls and strolled around.

alone, utterly alone, between
the Trojans and Achaeans, feeling the wind pressing my fine veils
against me, brushing my nipples, embracing my whole body
both clothed and naked, with only a single wide silver belt
holding my breasts up high—

there I was, beautiful, untouched, experienced
while my two rivals in love were dueling and the fate of the long war
was being determined—

I didn't even see the strap of Paris' helmet
severed— instead I saw a brightness from its brass,
a circular brightness, as his opponent swung it in rage
around his head— an illumined zero.

It wasn't really worth looking at—
the will of the gods had shaped things from the start; and Paris,
divested of his dusty sandals, would soon be in bed,

cleansed by the hands of the goddess, waiting for me, smirking,
pretentiously hiding a false scar on his side with a pink bandage.
I didn't watch anymore; hardly even listened to their war-cries—
I, high up on the walls, over the heads of mortals, airy, carnate,
belonging to no one, needing no one
as though I were (I, independent) absolute Love— free
from the fear of death and time, with a white flower in my hair,
with a flower between my breasts, and another in between my lips
    hiding for me
the smile of freedom.
                    They could have shot
their arrows at me from either side.
                    I was an easy target
walking slowly on the walls, completely etched
against the golden crimson of the evening sky.
                    I kept my eyes closed
to make any hostile gesture easy for them— knowing deeply
that none of them would dare. Their hands trembled with awe
at my beauty and immortality—
                    (maybe I can elaborate on that:
I didn't fear death because I felt it was so far from me).
                                        Then
I tossed down the two flowers from my hair and breasts— keeping
    the third one
in my mouth— I tossed them down from both sides of the wall
with an absolutely impartial gesture.
                    Then the men, both within and without,
threw themselves upon each other, enemies and friends, to snatch
the flowers, to offer them to me— my own flowers. I didn't see
anything else after that— only bent backs, as if all of them
were kneeling on the ground, where the sun was drying the blood—
    maybe

they had even crushed the flowers.
                I didn't see.
                                I'd raised my arms
and risen on the tips of my toes, and ascended
letting the third flower also drop from my lips.

All this remains with me still— a sort of consolation, a remote
    justification, and perhaps
this will remain, I hope, somewhere in the world— a momentary freedom,
illusory too of course— a game of our luck and our ignorance. In
    precisely
that position (as I recall), the sculptors worked on
my last statues; they're still out there in the garden;
you must have seen them when you came in. Sometimes I also (when
    the servants are in good spirits
and hold me by my arms to take me to that chair
in front of the window), I also can see them. They glow in the sun-
light. A white heat
wafts from the marble right up here. I won't dwell on it any
    longer.
It tires me out too after awhile. I'd rather watch a part of the
    street
where two or three kids play with a rag ball, or some girl
lowers a basket on a rope from the balcony across the way.
Sometimes the servants forget I'm there. They don't come to put
    me back in bed.
I stay all night gazing at an old bicycle, propped up
in front of the lit window of a new candy store,
until the lights go out, or I fall asleep on the window-sill.
    Every now

and then I think that a star wakes me, falling through space
like the saliva from a toothless, slack mouth of an old man.
Now
it's been ages since they've taken me to the window. I stay here in
bed
sitting up or lying down— I can handle that. To pass the time
I grasp my face— an unfamiliar face— touch it, feel it, count
the hairs, the wrinkles, the warts— who's inside
this face?
Something acrid rises in my throat— nausea and fear,
a silly fear, my God, that even the nausea might be lost. Stay
for awhile—
a little light's coming through the window— they must have lit the
street lamps.

Wouldn't you like me to ring for something for you?— some
preserved cherries
or candied bitter orange— maybe something's left in the big jars,
turned to congealed sugar by now— if, of course the greedy servants
have left anything. The last few years I've been busy
making sweets— what else is there to do?
After Troy— life in Sparta
was very dull— really provincial; shut up all day at home,
among the crowded spoils of so many wars; and memories,
faded and annoying, sneaking up behind you in the mirror
as you combed your hair, or in the kitchen emerging
from the greasy vapors of the pot; and you hear in the water's
boiling
a few dactylic hexameters from the Third Rhapsody
as a cock crows discordantly, close by, from a neighbor's coop.

You surely know how humdrum our life is. Even the newspapers
have the same shape, size, headlines— I no longer read them.
    Over and over
flags on balconies, national celebrations, parades
of toy soldiers— only the cavalry maintained something improvised,
something personal— maybe because of the horses. The dust rose
    like a cloud;
we closed the window— afterward you'd have to go about dusting,
    piece by piece,
vases, little boxes, picture frames, small porcelain statues,
    mirrors, buffets.
I stopped going to the celebrations. My husband used to come
    back sweating,
fling himself on his food, licking his chops, re-chewing
old, boring glories and resentments gone up in smoke. I stared at
his waistcoat buttons which were about to pop— he'd become quite
    fat.
Under his chin a large black stain flickered.

Then I'd prop my chin up, distractedly, continuing my meal,
feeling my lower jaw move in my hand
as though it were detached from my head, and I was holding it naked
    in my palm.
Maybe because of this I got fat too. I don't know. Everybody seemed
    scared—
I saw them sometimes from the windows— walking on a slant,
sort of limping, as though they were concealing something under
    their arms. Afternoons
the bells range dismally. The beggars knocked on the doors. In the
    distance

as night fell, the white-washed façade of the Maternity Hospital
seemed whiter,
farther away and unknowable. We lit the lamps quickly. I'd alter
an old dress. Then the sewing machine broke down; they took it
into the basement with those old romantic oil paintings
full of banal mythical scenes— Aphrodites rising from the sea,
Eagles and Ganymedes.

One by one our old acquaintances left. The mail diminished.
Only a brief postcard for special occasions, birthdays—
a stereotyped scene of Mount Taygetos with ridged peaks, very blue,
a part of the Eurotas river with white pebbles and rhododendrons,
or the ruins of Mistras with wild fig trees. But more often,
telegrams of condolences. No answers came. Maybe
the recipient had died in the meantime— we don't get news anymore.

My husband traveled no more. Didn't open a book. In his later
years
he grew very nervous. He smoked incessantly. Strolled around at
nights
in the huge living room, with those tattered brown slippers
and his long nightgown. At noon, at the table, he'd bring up
memories
of Clytemnestra's infidelity and how right Orestes' actions were
as though he were threatening someone. Who cared? I didn't even
listen. Yet
when he died, I missed him much— I missed most of all his silly
threats,
as though they'd frozen me into an immobile position in time,

as though they'd prevented me from becoming old.
Then I used to dream
of Odysseus, he too with the same agelessness, with his smart
triangular cap,
delaying his return, that crafty guy— with the pretence of imaginary
dangers,
whereas he'd throw himself (supposedly ship-wrecked) at times in
the arms of a Circe, at times in the arms
of a Nausicaa, to have the barnacles taken off his chest, to be
bathed
with small bars of rose soap, to have the scar on his knee kissed,
to be anointed with oil.

I think he also reached Ithaca— dull, fat Penelope must have muffled
him up
in those things she weaves. I never got a message from him since
then—
the servants might have torn them up— what does it matter anymore?
The Symblygades
shifted to another more inner place— you can feel them
immobile, softened— worse than ever— they don't crush,
they drown you in a thick, black fluid— nobody escapes them.
You may go now. Night's fallen. I'm sleepy. Oh, to close my eyes,
to sleep, to see nothing outside or inside, to forget
the fear of sleeping and awakening. I can't. I jump up—
I'm afraid I'll never wake again. I stay up, listening to
the snoring of the servants from the living room, the spiders on
the walls,
the cockroaches in the kitchen, the dead snoring
with deep inhalations, as though sound asleep, calmed down.
Now I'm even losing my dead. I've lost them. They're gone.

Sometimes, after midnight, the rhythmic hoofbeats of the horses
of a late carriage can be heard, as though they are returning
from a dismal show of some broken-down theatre in the neighborhood
with its plaster fallen from the ceiling, its peeling walls,
its enormous faded red curtain drawn,
shrunken from too many washings, leaving a space below
to reveal the bare feet of the great stage manager or the electrician
maybe rolling up a paper forest so the lights can be shut off.

That crack is still alight, while in the auditorium
the applause and the chandeliers are long since vanished. The air
is heavy with the breath of silence, the hum of silence beneath
the empty seats together with the shells from sunflower seeds and
    twisted-up tickets,
a few buttons, a lace handkerchief, and a piece of red string.

... And that scene, on the walls of Troy— did I really undergo an
    ascension,
letting fall from my lips— ? Sometimes even now,
as I lie here in bed, I try to raise my arms, to stand
on tiptoe— to stand on air— the third flower—

(She stopped talking. Her head fell back. She might have been asleep. The other person got up. He didn't say Good-night. Darkness had already come. As he went out into the corridor, he felt the servants glued to the wall, eavesdropping. Motionless. He went down the stairs as though into a deep well, with the feeling that he wouldn't find any exit – any door. His fingers, contracted, search for the doorknob. He even imagined that his hands were two birds gasping for want of air, yet knowing at the same time that this was no more than the expression of self-pity which we usually compare with vague fear. Suddenly voices were heard from upstairs. The electric lights were turned on in the corridor, on the stairs, in the rooms. He went up again. Now he was sure. The woman was sitting on the bed with her elbow propped up on the tin table, her cheek resting in her palm. The servants were noisily going in an out. Somebody was making a phone call in the hall. The women in the neighborhood rushed in. 'Ah, ah,' they cried, as they hid things under their dresses. Another phone call. Already the police were coming up. They sent the servants and the women away, but the neighbors had time to grab the bird cages with the canaries, some flower pots with exotic plants, a transistor, an electric heater. One of them grabbed a gold picture frame. They put the dead woman onto a stretcher. The person in charge sealed up the house – 'until the rightful owners are found,' he said – although he knew there weren't any. The house would stay like that, sealed up for forty days, and after, its possessions – as many as were saved – would be auctioned off for the public good. 'To the morgue,' he said to the driver. The covered car went off. Everything suddenly disappeared. Total silence. He was alone. He turned and looked around. The moon had risen. The statues in the garden were dimly lit – her statues, solitary, beside the trees, outside of the closed house. And a silent, deceitful moon. Where could he go now?).

May – August, 1970

THE T.E. LAWRENCE POEMS

1982

Water

When you think of it, water is everything. Or rather,
Water ventures into everything and becomes everything.
                    It has
All tastes and moods imaginable; water is history
And the end of the world is water also.
                                        I have tasted water
From London to Miranshah. In France it tasted
Of Crusaders' breastplates, swords, and tunnels of rings
On ladies' fingers.
                    In the springs of Lebanon water had
No colour, and was therefore all colours,
                                          outside of Damascus
It disguised itself as snow and let itself be chopped
And spooned onto the stunned red grapes of summer.

For years I have defended water, even though I am told
          there are other drinks.
Water will never lie to you, even when it insinuates itself
Into someone else's territory. Water has style.

Water has no conscience and no shame; water
          thrives on water, is self-quenching.
It often tastes of brine and ammonia, and always
Knows its way back home.

When you want to travel very far, do as the Bedouin do—
Drink to overflowing when you can,
                                        and then
Go sparingly between wells.

Our Child Which Art in Heaven

The child leads the parents on to bear him; he demands
to be born. And I sense somehow that God
Is not yet born; I want to create Him.

If everything were finished, and we could say
we'd given birth to stars, if we could say
Give over, it's done— all would be wild, and fair.

But it is not yet over; it has not yet begun.

God is not yet born, and we await the long scream
of His coming. We want the water to break
So we can say: *In the Beginning was the Word.*

Meanwhile, if one must die for something,
there's nothing like the cross
from which to contemplate the world.

Animal Spirits

Is it true, then, that one fears all that one loves?
These spirits are my awful companions, I can't tell
anyone when they move in me.
They are so mighty they are unclean; it is the end
Of cleanliness; it is the great crime.

I can only kill them by becoming them. They are all
I have ever loved or wanted; their hooves and paws
smell of honey and trodden flowers.

Those who do not know me sip their bitter coffee
        and mutter of war. They do not know
        I am wrestling with the spirits
        and have almost won. They do not know
I am looking out from the camels' eyes, out
        from the eyes of the horses.

It is vile to love them; I will not love them.
                                        Look—
My brain is sudden and silent as a wildcat.
                                        Lord,
Teach me to be lean, and wise. Nothing matters,
        nothing matters.

Tall Tales

It has been said that I sometimes lie, or bend the truth
to suit me. did I make that four hundred mile
trip alone in Turkish territory or not?
I wonder if it is anybody's business
to know. Syria is still there,
and the long lie that the war was.

Was there a poster of me offering money for my capture,
and did I stand there staring at myself,
daring anyone to know me? Consider
truth and untruth, consider why they call them
the *theatres* of war. All of us
played our roles to the hilt.

Poets only play with words, you know; they too
are masters of the Lie, the Grand Fiction.
Poets and men like me who fight for something
contained in words, but no words.

What if the whole show was a lie, and it bloody well was—
would I still lie to you? Of course I would.

There Is No Place to Hide

Here is a famous world; I'm standing on a stage
With ten spotlights on me, talking about how I detest
    publicity. I stand there like an ass,
    apologizing for having a past, a soul,
    a name (which one?), and then
    back shyly into the limelight.

No. What I'm really doing is standing in an unlit room
Holding a court martial upon myself. Shaw tells me
    that to live under a cloud
    is to defame God. I can neither reveal myself
    nor hide. No matter what I do, I am naked.
I can clothe myself in silk or chain mail, and I
    am naked; everything shows through
    and yet no one can see me.

Can you imagine that posterity will call me wonderful
    on the basis of a few pencil sketches,
    a revolt in the desert,
    and my irresistably foul soul?
Outside my window, a small tit bird bashes itself
    against the glass. At first I thought
    it was admiring itself in the window.
    Now I know it's mad.

Notes from the Dead Land

I have died at last, Feisal. I have been lying
On this hospital bed for five days, and I know
        that I am dead. I was going back home
        on my big bike, and I wasn't doing more
        than sixty when this black van, death camel,
Slid back from the left side of my head, and ahead,
Two boys on little bikes were biking along, and
        something in my head, some brutal music
        played on and on. I was going too fast,
        I was always going too fast for the world,
So I swerved and fell on my stupid head, right
In the middle of the road. I addressed myself
        to the dark hearts of the tall trees
        and nothing answered.

The Arabs say that when you pray, two angels stand
On either side of you, recording good and bad deeds,
        and you should acknowledge them.
        Lying here, I decide that now
        the world can have me any way it pleases.
I will celebrate my perfect death here. *Maktub*:
It is written. I salute both of the angels.

– Behold part of the violent skies...
Gwendolyn

NOMAN'S LAND

1985

WAS GOING TO BE A WRITER
—when the
brown
She would not find the poems there. With no one to
Street West, near the
Harry Blackstone make everything disap-
and pimps hung out at Wah Mai—when the

THE LONELIEST COUNTRY IN THE WORLD

He was lost. And he was naked, wet and shivering. He was lost in a rain-drenched midnight Eden, and all the black trees around him were whispering like mad and laughing. Thunder blossomed in the distance.

And something else was very wrong. Then he remembered: he'd lost his memory.

Oh damn, he thought, and flung himself through the underbrush. After a time the forest surrendered to the road which glistened like a strip of licorice in the rain. He leaned against a tree and remembered that he had passed under an arch of blinding light, and been struck down by a hand of fire. Then, slowly, the smell of the earth, the awareness of his body, the certain knowledge that he had no idea who or where he was.

He blinked and headed for the road. The sleek metallic rain kept pouring down so his vision was blurred, but at one point he saw, or thought he saw, something which made his blood run cold. It was a huge neon sign shimmering in shades of blue and green. It hovered for a moment over the forest, then disappeared. WELCOME, it read, TO THE LONELIEST COUNTRY IN THE WORLD.

I'll hitch a ride to somewhere, he thought. *But how can I? I'm naked!*

Since it was early Spring the forest was still quite bare, but scattered here and there were a few of last year's maple leaves. They lay on the ground in what had once been wanton splendour; originally they had been golden-red, but now they were dirty orange, shades of rust. He found that he could peel them off of the ground like soggy pages of the earth's diary, layers of its skin. He chose one of the largest and held it over the nakedest part of his nakedness. Then he stepped to the edge of the road and held up his thumb. *At least I remember how to thumb a ride; that means I'll remember lots of things later.*

A small red car shot out of the night and came to a screeching stop beside him. The driver, a woman, leaned out of the window and stared at him in disbelief. She was very beautiful; he wanted to die. *She thinks I'm some kind of pervert. But wait – would a pervert be clad in a maple leaf? I'm going to assume control of this situation.*

'Excuse me, Miss,' he said, 'I'm in need of help. I've lost three things: I've lost my way, I've lost my clothes, and I've lost my memory.'

'Your *memory?*' she asked. 'Oh come on!'

'It's true, I swear it.'

'Do you mean you have amnesia?'

'Yes, and I'm also catching a cold.'

She began to laugh. It was an unusual laugh; it was almost as though she were laughing in another language.

'Well, if you feel it's that funny, I'll take another car!' he said, offended. 'I have my pride,' he added, clutching the leaf to his groin. 'And I'm in no hurry.'

She opened the door for him. 'It's all right. Come in then, stranger.' She reached over into the back seat and produced an old brown blanket bordered by a geometric Indian pattern; gratefully, he draped it around himself as best he could in a style resembling a toga.

'You wouldn't have a pin or a clasp to hold this thing together?' he asked.

She pulled something from her hair which was made from a sweep of turquoise feathers and shell and bone. With some difficulty he manoeuvred it through the coarse material of the blanket so the toga was fastened at the shoulder. Then he saw that her black hair had fallen free, and it was straight and shiny, and although she wasn't laughing anymore there was a maddening little smile around the corners of her mouth.

'Now,' she said, when they had turned from the road in the forest onto the highway, 'tell me about yourself.'

'But I can't! There's nothing to tell; I don't know who I am!'

'Oh come on!'

'Why would I invent such a story? I don't know where my clothes are, I don't know where I was going, and I don't know what happened to my memory."

'Cigarette?' she asked, pointing to a pack of Export on the dashboard.

'I don't smoke,' he said, then frowned. 'What am I saying? 'Of course I smoke.' And he helped himself to a cigarette.

'For the time being I'll go along with you,' she said, casting him a long sideways glance. 'I'll assume you're telling the absolute truth.'

'I swear it, I swear it.' He coughed loudly and put out the cigarette in the crowded ashtray. 'I don't smoke,' he added, and sank back into the brown depths of the toga.

'And you don't remember *anything?*'

'Nothing. Except things like night and day, heat and cold, how to speak.'

She was worried now, not smiling. 'There was a huge electric storm back there. Maybe you were struck by lightning.'

'I felt a hand of fire,' he said, 'here, just across my left shoulder. It sort of slapped me down. And my whole left arm is numb.'

There was a long silence as the miles whizzed by.

'Back there...' he said finally, 'you say *back there* and I realize that I don't know what you mean. Back where? I mean – where are we?'

'Back there was a place called Kingsmere,' she informed him, 'the residence of a former prime minister of this country. We are not far from Ottawa, capital of this country.'

He liked the way she drove; she didn't clutch the wheel like he pictured other drivers doing, as though they expected it to assume a demonic will of its own and steer itself into oblivion; her right elbow on her lap, she guided the car with the merest touch of her fingertips on the bottom of the wheel. Almost no other cars were on the highway, and as they rolled on through the night with the broad thunder receding in the distance, they might have been anywhere in the world.

'I don't want to sound like a fool,' he said, drumming his fingers against the dashboard, 'but— may I take another cigarette? I think I do smoke— but, when you say *this country* I honestly don't know where you mean.'

'Oh *come on!*'

'I'm serious. I don't know where you mean.'

'This country,' she said slowly, 'is called Kanada.'

'Oh. Kanada.'

The second cigarette tasted better than the first. He finished it and fell asleep.

He awoke sighing and talking to himself the way sleepers do when they leave the private country of their sleep. 'Where are we going?' he murmured.

'Toronto. Unless you have some other place in mind.'

She told him that her name was Kali, and that she had an extra room in her little house in the east end of the city; he was welcome to stay there for a day or two until he recovered his memory.

'You're not afraid of me? You don't even know my name. For that matter, neither do I.'

'Then for the moment,' she replied, 'I'll call you *Noman.*'

The next time he slept it was in a voluptuous bed under a dark red cover that felt like heavy ancient velvet. He prayed to the Unknown God – the only god who came to mind, an ideal god for a man in his condition – to give him his memory back. But he woke up the following morning with the flu; the cold wet night in the forest had lowered his resistance to the world. He lay in bed with a high fever, and Kali made him lemon tea and Marmite sandwiches; now and again she tried to distract him with a page or two of escapist fiction or nature poetry, but he tossed and turned and refused to be entertained. Once, in his despair he tried to eat the pillow, and when he saw the lost feathers floating in the air he declared that his mind was a cloud, a snowstorm; he talked of the wings of the angel of death, which were not black, but white.

The second night he woke up drenched in sweat, the bed was a lake of black water where he sank and drowned. He tried to crawl in between the folds of the magnificent suffocating cover and disappear among the layers of dreams that lay between this world and the other.

'Kali,' he said, his face a gruesome mushroom grey, 'I want to be sure that my precious parts go to Science. My brain to the General Hospital in – where was it? – Ottawa. My eyes to Mount Sinai, my heart—'

'There are far worse things than having the flu,' she said, and brought him the fiftieth pot of lemon tea.

'Like what?' He stared at the Japanese maidens on the teapot, walking back and forth over the same bridge, forever.

'You could be lame, paralyzed, blind. You could be a leper, or a mythopoeic poet.'

'I'll drink the tea.'

'Not to mention what fearful diseases of the spirit, or even of your immortal soul.'

'I'll drink the tea!' he cried, his arms outstretched in wild pursuit of the Japanese maidens.

That day the fever played itself out, and the next day as she was standing in front of the hall mirror she turned to see him framed in the doorway, about to go out, the outline of his body fuzzy and unreal in the early morning light. Behind him the blue-grey haze of the strange city rose from his shoulders like wings.

'Kali, who am I?' he whispered, and he was afraid. '*Who am I?*'

He wanted to break every rule in the world, to commit unspeakable but perfectly reasonable acts in an effort to find himself; everything was within his reach, everything was impossible. Surely she knew how desperate he was? But she said nothing; she was absorbed in the complex ritual of braiding her hair and tying it into place. He resisted the urge to shake her so it all came apart again.

'Then who are you? You live alone here. Do you have a family? Do you have a man?'

'I did.'

'And where is he? What happened to him?'

'Oh,' she said, 'he died.'

'I'm sorry,' he said, and of course he wasn't.

'So am I.' *We ploughed through each other's lives,* she thought, *leaving these furrows a mile wide, these great gashes in each other's souls.*

'What was he like?' He wondered if he should be asking all these questions.

A kaleidoscope, a collage, a creature who occupied the spaces between moments, sliding in between the folds of reality, his life a room composed of sliding panels and doors.

'He was quite unusual,' she said.

He studied her. She was not, as he had first thought, beautiful; she was slim and angular. One of her ancestors was a Mohawk, she had told him. When she spoke, her voice took on a low conspiratorial tone as though she had just escaped from a situation that was fraught with danger, or was about to embark on a madly daring and clandestine escapade. Every word was charged with a dark, quiet excitement. In moments of ecstasy or distress, he was to learn later, she insisted on fleeing to India but never went. Although she had travelled in the past she now got no farther than packing her bags. She had told him that she often had trouble deciding which aspect of herself to present to the world— the North American Indian resplendent with beads and feathers, or that other Indian after whom she was named, the dusky and terrible consort of Siva, Kali.

'I'm going out,' he announced. 'But first tell me about that place where you found me. What is this Kingsmere?'

'Kingsmere was the residence of Prime Minister William Lyon Mackenzie King. Short, fat little man with a brown suit and a little dog. If you study a picture of him it's like studying a snowbank: opaque, inscrutable. He communicated telepathically with his dog, employed mediums to contact his dead mother, and made no important decisions unless the hands of a clock or watch formed a propitious angle. He needed spiritualists, he needed prostitutes. He had dreams and visions of Hitler and was impressed by the Fuehrer's "love of peace."'

'Baffling man,' said Noman.

'He imported pseudo Graeco-Roman columns and bits and pieces from historic buildings and used them to decorate the grounds at Kingsmere. Zap— instant history. But he was wrong; all he did was create a sort of grotesque stage set. But for what play? The place is surreal, with all those arches leading nowhere but to the forest. He tried to decorate the present with relics from the past, and ended up creating a time-warp. The ruins don't belong in that landscape, the landscape rejects them, they create a tension that's almost electrically charged.' She glanced at his arm, recovered now from the numbing effect of the lightning.

'Is there anything you can tell me about this country that I should know now, before I set out? It doesn't seem quite real to me.'

'Nor to anyone!' she laughed. 'Nor will it ever, until we look inside of what's real to discover what's *real.* The dark myths of the forest. And it won't settle into time, into history, until we know it well enough to make fiction of it, to play with it. Until we take it so seriously we can stop taking it seriously. There is another country, you know, and it's inside this one.' She tied something blue onto her braids.

'What was I doing at Kingsmere the night you found me?' he asked.

'You tell me.'

'I *can't*!'

She went into the kitchen and left him to rendezvous with himself in the mirror. If he had been born, so to speak, at Kingsmere – could he be a reincarnation of the madcap King? But he had no particular fondness for dogs, and politics distressed and bored him. He studied himself in the glass. He was probably in his mid-forties, or so his general condition, including that of his teeth – two extractions, several fillings – indicated. He was fairly tall, with a lean and muscular build; it was the body (perhaps) of a dancer or a runner, of someone accustomed to long, lyrical exercise involving endurance and coordination. Dark auburn hair, eyes that changed colour, nationality uncertain. As for his naked self, which had surprised him that morning in the bath, there was an egg-shaped birthmark on his inner thigh and a small scar from some operation on his abdomen; his skin had a faintly olive cast. He had found that he couldn't wear a watch because his pulse interfered with it somehow and made it stop. Kali had given him one belonging to her late boyfriend (as did the clothes he now wore), and the thing gave up on him each time he put it on. Private time subverting world time, he mused.

Who was he? Useless scraps of information, names, places, random data, combined to form nothing he could call a memory. He had no family, he was sure; no one was related to him. Someone had stolen his passport to life, if indeed he ever had a passport. Or else he was merely something that someone had misplaced, someone who was now rummaging through papers in a desk in the Library of Lost Souls in search of him.

He couldn't be sure of anything; of that he was certain. There were no truths, no lies. Everything was very important.

'Well, I'm going out,' he called, and returned to the doorway.

'Do you want me to go with you?' She came out, holding two glasses of orange juice.

'No.'

'I've got to clean these windows,' she said, running a finger down the pane of glass in the door. Then she drew a lion through the film of dirt, and he drew a bird and a dolphin. 'Good luck out there,' she added.

'I don't want luck. I want a past, I want a second name, a social insurance number, a soul.'

'You already have a soul.'

'I've never been introduced to my soul. Souls are cheap. I want to smash this window, I want to fly, I want to write a sequel to the *Odyssey*, I want to die, I want to swim the lake, I want to break all the rules there are and then make new ones so I can break them too, I want to invent electricity; my needs are simple.'

The world beyond the window as it looked now through the transparent bodies of the animals was a fabulous and terrifying place.

'You can do anything you like, then,' she said as their glasses clicked and kissed. 'There is the city.'

He went to the police and asked them if he was a Missing Person; he went to the library and looked himself up in *Who's Who's in Kanada* (he wasn't there); he gave two dollars to a girl with green hair in Yorkville who read his palm and told him that he was at a turning point in his life and things would either be good or bad; he almost wept for joy when a young man asked him, 'Do you want to know who you really are?' And he cried 'Yes, yes!' only to discover that he had inadvertently consented to take a Scientology test. He went to a psychiatrist who asked him about his sex life, and he replied that he'd never had one, and anyway he was only six days old. By the end of the week he was exhausted and feeling a little reckless, which was why suddenly, at the corner of Yonge and Bloor, he grabbed the violin from the hands of a young street musician who played there every day, found the instrument familiar and satisfying, and immediately gave forth a brilliant rendition of Rimsky-Korsakov's *Hymn to the Sun.* He felt better afterwards.

He kept dreaming he was swimming in a huge lake with the shoreline nowhere in sight, and it occurred to him that this probably meant that he wanted to swim, so he went to the nearest pool and realized immediately that he was indeed a superb swimmer. His body rejoiced in itself; he did fifteen lengths in an excellent crawl with scarcely any effort. Then he did fifteen more. Afterwards in the shower room he surprised his naked fellow swimmers by breaking out into boisterous lines of Homeric poetry, in the original Greek. Soon he found a job as a lifeguard in a high-school pool which was creamy white like old porcelain or a dentist's bowl, streaked along the sides with slippery yellow. In the evening he taught a group of students called the Water Babies, and standing with them, waist-deep in the blinking turquoise water, he told them that swimming was just like navigating in dreams. 'Open your eyes underwater!' he cried. 'What are you afraid to see down there— yourselves?' And when the lessons were over he'd circle the pool and peer into the depths for lost engagement rings, band-aids, jewels. He quit smoking and breathed.

He moved into a room on the third floor of a house close to the lake. It was an odd, circular room with windows looking out in three directions. He called it the tower room. It had silly orange curtains that whizzed across the windows on long metal runners. There was a magic tree outside – Ygdrasil. Marvellous children made hopscotch marks all over the sidewalk in purple and white chalk. Small kids didn't sit on the cerbs after sundown because then the black asphalt became a river, and something call Orca swam down it to bite off their feet. It was wonderful; there were no limits to the world.

Some buildings had signs on them saying JERUSALEM, CAIRO', ATHENS and so on. It was part of a festival called Caravan.

You could start off the day with ordinary cornflakes, watch native dancers twirl and beat drums all morning, have a lunch of Lebanese falafel, buy Russian embroidery and Spanish dolls in the afternoon, have Italian pasta and Brio for dinner, take in Ukrainian dances in the evening and wind up with Chinese food at midnight, having seen only one or two token Anglo Saxons all day. You had no idea whose country you were in; it was perfectly Kanadian. It was wonderful. He had never been so lonely.

He began walking around everywhere, looking for his life. In Eatons, everything was inside out; indoors was made to look like outdoors with real trees and fake avenues. He got into a transparent elevator with women who wore black lipstick and musk perfume that turned men into animals. A memory seized him in a stranglehold around the throat; he was in the Eatons of the Forties in an elevator where a woman in a navy-blue suit with white cuffs and immaculate white gloves was opening and closing the metal gates that moved like accordions and calling out the floors in a nasal monotone. When the memory released its grip he was left with the image of a white disembodied glove floating in the air, and the sound of sliding metal doors.

But whatever else it was, it was a charmed life. Often he'd find himself on some unknown street, staring in disbelief as suddenly everything before his eyes began to shimmer and glow with a frightening radiance. The hallucinatory *presence* of things. The trees, the grass, the sidewalk seemed on the brink of confessing to him and him alone their luminous secrets. Confronting the miraculous, he could only shake his head and whisper *look at this, look at this,* as a kind of delicious terror gripped him and he was consumed by something he called godfire. But he was also cursed with an awful inclusive vision, the painful ability to see everything at once. Thus the darkness alongside of the radiance, and the sight of his fellow human beings in their pathetic and hilarious attempts to be beautiful, to be important, to be immortal, drove him into a quietness which was at all times between laughter and tears.

And nobody knew him; the high-heeled woman who strode back and forth across the city in purple suede boots, taking up the whole sidewalk, her whole being in pursuit of some lavish dream, didn't know him; the Greeks carrying around the unbearable burden of their own existence didn't know him; the woman known as the Swedish Queen who wore pink harem pants and outrageous jewellery and a gold ribbon that said SOCIALISM across her chest didn't know him; the Chinese and Jamaicans and Hungarians and Philipinos didn't know him; the bag ladies didn't know him; the troubled young woman who cut up playing cards and left the pieces on the pavement in front of churches and police stations in some sort of private ritual didn't know him. (One morning he picked up a part of the Three of Diamonds and spent an hour looking for the rest because perhaps she was trying to communicate with him by means of a secret code.)

Kali, he thought (this in the darkest nights), *I am so lonely.*

He walked all over the city, talking to popcorn vendors from places like Lisbon and Gibraltar and Corinth, to newspaper boys and mailmen and street cleaners. He wore a light brown trenchcoat, and because he looked like such a gentleman and spoke so softly and politely when he asked people if they knew who he was, they often dismissed the idea that he might be mad and were almost sorry that, no, they didn't know him and never had. Finally it was clear to him that nobody knew him and why should they? The world was theirs – or was it? Were they also alone? Was this city somebody's rough diagram of reality, or was it pure mirage? He gazed at the Tower – tallest free-standing structure in the world – and it shimmered in the gray air, a monument to nothing, a spaceship that would never have lift-off, a rocket without a launching pad.

They didn't know who they were, so they came and built these big cities in the wilderness. They still found it empty, so they stuck up this tower in the emptiness. They were so lonely they didn't even know it, maybe even lonelier than me.

On one of his walks he learned that he possessed certain magical powers which, although feeble and uneven at first, held promise of greater things to come. The simplest of these powers and the one which was easiest to summon up was telekinesis, and he passed some pleasant moments moving small objects such as pebbles back and forth across the sidewalk. But he soon tired of this, impatient for more dramatic feats.

News made no sense to him because he had no backdrop against which the world's daily drama might be played. He swam and swam and watched the fishy bodies of the other swimmers thrashing around, their vision coloured by red and green goggles, or crawling back and forth doing lengths, doing lengths, covering the same ground over and over like his futile thoughts. Yet there was a seductive loneliness about swimming; the water was easy, opening for him and permitting him passage, offering no resistance. Too easy, he thought. What he needed were huge waves bashing his head, black angry ones whipped up by wind, brutal cold ones thick with froth and plankton from the mouths of seabeasts, waves so chilled and merciless they would pour through the sluice gates of his memory. Not this tame pool he swam in daily, this tepid water. When he showered down after his swim, splashing off the layers of chlorine and blinking the turquoise film from his eyes, the porcelain tiles on the walls of the shower room were as white and vapid as his memory; they were like nascent photographs in a chemical solution waiting to develop. But no image ever appeared on them. *At least I have an open mind,* he told himself. *In your condition,* said a familiar and increasingly perverse voice in his head, *what other kind could you have?*

In the tower room he went to bed early and listened to the tic-toc of bedsprings coming from somewhere in the old house where lovers were creating their own love-clock, a challenge to ordinary-time.

(Everyone was perishing from loneliness except the lovers. Everyone was walking around with a list of loves and terrors in his head, hoping to meet somebody with an identical list. Looking for sibling images, flirting with mirrors.) But mostly he listened to the lake when it grew stormy and the crashing of lakewaves, south of his head, against the breakwater.

Kali was a costume designer for a small theatre company which was doing a new version of *The Cyclops.* At a theatre party he met a lot of people who all seemed to be talking about the Alexander Technique and their recent trips to Crete. 'I saw one guy from New York arguing with a café owner who'd said, quite nicely, how he liked to please the foreigners,' one man said, 'and the guy turned on him shouting *I'm not foreign, I'm American!* Now a Kanadian would never think of saying that, you know?' He also learned at the party that in Crete people still Tilled the Soil. And the editor of *The Golden Yo-Yo: A Magazine of the Arts* declared to anyone within range of his voice that regional theatre was dead. Noman listened, baffled.

The next week he went to see the play, and one of the actors delivered a line that made his blood run cold. Sweat broke out on his forehead; it seemed to him that everyone in the audience turned toward him. *Jesus Christ, they're doing a play about me,* he thought, and went to the nearest bar and drank himself into oblivion. He wrote NOMAN WAS HERE on the washroom wall, and considered it to be the most suggestive and obscene piece of graffiti ever composed. At two-thirty in the morning Kali got a call from a police station informing her that they were holding a drunk they'd picked up on Bay Street who claimed he knew her. He kept saying, 'Noman they call me, my father and mother, and all my fellows.'

She picked him up from the station and drove him back to the tower room. 'All right, Kali, I give up,' he said, because it was clear to him now that of course she had always known him. He was the man who had died. 'Tell me everything. Am I supposed to be dead, is that it? And if so— why?'

'Some people think you're dead; it's easier for them to deal with you when you're dead,' she said. 'But I wouldn't dwell on it.'

'Why didn't you tell me before?'

'When I knew you before you also claimed you had amnesia. It's your old trick.'

'This time it's no trick, I swear it. Aren't you going to tell me anything about the past?'

'Even if it's no trick... no. You had a thousand pasts. And anyway, if I wait long enough, you'll tell me. It'll come back to you in pieces.'

'Tell me *something!* Was I a murderer, or a poet? Was I rich, was I poor?'

'You weren't rich, you just lived like you were. I thought you were, until you sold everything in your apartment one day to pay off your debts. That was a while ago. You've been away rather a long time.'

'How long? Tell me *something.* What do I love?'

'Mathematics, music, Metaxa brandy, astronomy.'

'What do I fear?'

'The last hour of the night – the hour of the wolf – albinos for some strange reason, comets, quicksilver, fireworks, the last hour of the day.'

'And?'

'No more. You were always inventing yourself; now you can do it again.'

The tower room loomed above him. He waited for a moment on the sidewalk and waved after her as she drove away. She watched him growing smaller and smaller in the rear-view mirror, moving back through private time, retreating into microcosms where all manner of pasts were possible, and therefore all manner of futures. She wondered if he knew how lucky he was. *Yes I know you,* she thought, *I know all about you— all the people you aren't, all the places you can't be found.*

That night it rained and rained. In the last hour of the night he couldn't sleep. He opened the shameless orange curtains, rust-coloured now by moonlight, and looked down onto the street. Some people were walking home, and their multi-coloured umbrellas were codified dots in a computer's memory – *the codes of yesterday,* he thought, *the codes of possible tomorrows* – or bingo chips, or the dots of those crazy modern clocks which had no numbers or hands and lit up in key positions to tell the time. Beyond the street with its anonymous residents, down a steep hill and over an expressway, the lake heaved and sighed. The funny green dinosaurs and purple monsters in the children's playground on the lakeshore were getting drenched in the rain. He stared out, feeling suddenly very afraid. The rain slid down diagonal slots from the sky, the fat trees lurched like drunkards in the wind, the magic tree outside the window shone like a star. The street was a glistening strip of licorice; it became a road in the Gatineau hills. It was the first day of the world, and he was naked and alone.

But he started to fall asleep despite himself. The rain turned into an angel timidly knocking on the doors of his consciousness, then it was a horseman pounding on the door of an inn in Italy in the fifteenth century. Then as he sank into the dark waters of deeper sleep he thought he would die here in this loneliest of countries.

Whose country, what country? For that matter, what world? His mind was at an oblique angle, leaning into nowhere. The darkness drove a wedge into his reason. The wind confided in him all through the last hour of the night, telling him its obscure troubles. He knew that he couldn't face this loneliness much longer. He also knew that he would have to.

AFTERWORLDS

1987

The Grand Dance

I promised I would never turn you into poetry, but
Allow this liar these wilful, wicked lines.

I am simply trying to track you down
In preworlds and afterworlds
And the present myriad inner worlds
Which whirl around in the carousel of space.

I hurl breathless poems against my lord Death,
Send these words, these words
Careening into the beautiful darkness.

And where do all the words go?
They say that somewhere out there in space
Every word uttered by every man
Since the beginning of man
Is still sounding. Afterthoughts,

Lethal gossip of the spheres.

Dance then, dance in the city streets,
Your body a fierce illusion of flesh, of energy,
The particles of light cast off from your hair
Illumine you for this moment only.

Your afterimage claims the air
And every moment is Apocalypse—

Avatar, deathless
Anarchy.

The White Horse

This is the first horse to come into the world;
It heaved itself out of the sea to stand now
In a field of dizzy sunlight,
Its eyes huge with joy and wisdom,
Its head turned towards you, wondering
          why you are wondering

And how it comes about that you are here, when
Shrapnel from wars whose causes are forgotten
Has invaded the soft legs and bellies of children
And phosphorous bombs have made burnt ivory
          of the limbs of lovers
In Ireland and Lebanon and all the broken countries
Of the universe where this horse has never been.

You reach out your hand to touch it, and
This is the first time you have ever seen
          your hand, as it is also
The first time you have smelled the blue fire
Within a stone, or tasted blue air, or
Heard what the sea says when it talks in its sleep.

But hasn't the brilliant end come, you wonder,
And isn't the world still burning?

Go and tell this: It is morning,
And this horse with a mane the colour of seafoam
Is the first horse that the world has ever seen,
The white horse which stands now watching you
Across this field of endless sunlight.

Late Song

When it is all over – the crying and the dancing and the long
exhausting music – I will remember only
How once you flirted with your death and lifted your dark eyes
to warn me of the world's end
As wild leaves fell, and midnight crashed upon the city.

But it is never over; nothing ends until we want it to.
Look, in shattered midnights,
On black ice under silver trees, we are still dancing, dancing.

Meet me in an hour at the limits of the city.

The Death of the Loch Ness Monster

Consider that the thing has died before we proved it ever lived
    and that it died of loneliness, dark lord of the loch,
fathomless Worm, great Orm, this last of our mysteries—
    haifend ane meikill fin on ilk syde
    with ane taill and ane terribill heid—
and that it had no tales to tell us, only that it lived there,
    lake-locked, lost in its own coils,
waiting to be found; in the black light of midnight
    surfacing, its whole elastic length unwound,
and the sound it made as it broke the water
    was the single plucked string of a harp—
this newt or salamander, graceful as a swan,
    this water-snake, this water-horse, this water-dancer.

Consider him tired of pondering the possible existence of man
    whom he thinks he has sighted sometimes on the shore,
and rearing up from the purple churning water,
    weird little worm head swaying from side to side,
he denies the vision before his eyes;
    his long neck, swan of Hell, a silhouette against the moon
his green heart beating its last,
    his noble, sordid soul in ruins.

Now the mist is a blanket of doom, and we pluck from the depth
    a prize of primordial slime—
the beast who was born from some terrible ancient kiss,
    lovechild of unspeakable histories,
this ugly slug, half blind no doubt, and very cold,
    his head which is horror to behold

no bigger than our own;
no bigger than our own;
    whom we loathe, for his kind ruled the earth before us,
who died of loneliness in a small lake in Scotland,
    and in his mind's dark land,
where he dreamed up his luminous myths, the last of which was
    man.

The Garden of the Thieves

For years I have wanted to write a poem called
    The Garden of the Thieves.
The title turns up in old notebooks with asterisks
Surrounding it and arrows pointing to it, and
Notes telling me to write it, write it, but

It never got written until now because I never knew
    where the garden was, or who
The thieves were, so the naked title lay there
Between sheets of paper that seethed with reason
And grand ideas, until one night I actually dreamed

Of the garden where I played as a child, and it was
    invaded by *thieves*
Who stole the Great Poem from me, the one we all know
Never gets written, and I saw the title as they
Whisked it away, and yes, it was beyond a doubt

The Garden of the Thieves, written by Anonymous
    who was my favourite poet
And who I thought was a Byzantine king. I have been
Pondering over this for quite some time, and thought
I'd better get it all down before the night falls.

The Wah Mai Café

There's nothing new here; it's just how you pay for it.

Actually *it's* not here anymore, but it was
Near a theatre where blackstone made everything disappear
And an aging stripper made her tits circle simultaneously
In two opposite directions
And an androgynous angel they called Billy
Appeared at midnight.

So I'd go in my brown corduroy jumper and sit
And take notes because I Was Going To Be A Writer
And when one of the hookers Lily asked me what the hell
I was doing, I said I had to see the seamier side of life,
Etc. She said: You're OK, you can stay.

At the Wah Mai Café Lily would bum cigarettes off me
After she'd turned a trick down the lane
Until the night the cops raided the place and Lily said
Goodbye, Goodbye, as they took some pimps and hookers away.

Who the hell are you, one cop asked me, gazing in disbelief
At my brown corduroy jumper. I Am a Writer, I said,
And I work at Boys and Girls House which is
A children's library. Actually I'm just a page
But one day I'm going to be a Book.

For Christ's sake go home, said the cop, so I left
And I'm telling you, would I lie to you, it was wonderful

And awful, me and Lily and the others in the Wah Mai Café
All going out into the seamy night in opposite directions,
Some of them disappearing down the lane, me hopping a streetcar,

All of us trying to find our way back home.

Let Me Make This Perfectly Clear

Let me make this perfectly clear.
I have never written anything because it is a Poem.
This is a mistake you always make about me,
A dangerous mistake. I promise you
I am not writing this because it is a Poem.

You suspect this is a posture or an act.
I am sorry to tell you it is not an act.

You actually think I care if this
Poem gets off the ground or not. Well
I don't care if this poem gets off the ground or not
And neither should you.
All I have ever cared about
And all you should ever care about
Is what happens when you lift your eyes from this page.

Do not think for one minute it is the Poem that matters.
It is not the Poem that matters.
You can shove the Poem.
What matters is what is out there in the large dark
And in the long light,
Breathing.

But

Out there in the large dark and in the long light is the breathless
Poem,
As ruthless and beautiful and amoral as the world is,
As nature is.

In the end there's just me and the bloody Poem and the murderous
Tongues of the trees,
Their glossy green syllables licking my mind (the green
Work of the wind).

Out there in the night between two trees is the Poem saying:
Do not hate me
Because I peeled the veil from your eyes and tore your world
To shreds, and brought

The darkness down upon your head. Here is a book of tongues,
Take it. (Dark leaves invade the air.)
Beware! Now I know a language so beautiful and lethal
My mouth bleeds when I speak it.

Letters to Josef in Jerusalem

i

Josef, twenty years have passed since we sat in the cemetery
close to No Man's Land, on somebody's gravestone, in a
garden of death in Jerusalem, and the ancient night contained
our youth. Though we were younger and older than death,
and wise as the night was. All wars, we said, are born here
in the City of Peace, and Jerusalem is not a city but a whore;
thousands have taken her but she has only changed hands.

Do you remember

How the moonlight slayed us, its light a knife between our
ribs, and our knees and elbows gathered silver as we bowed
down. Yet we would not kneel in that most unholy of cities;
we sat on the eloquent stone watching the cats pass, apolitcal,
into No Man's Land. Only they ignored the borders,
only for them had the city never been divided. The washing
which had hung for centuries on the clotheslines was still
not dry, and

The Hebrew God was a string of names in the night.

Beneath the killing moonlight in the garden of tombstones,
you said that in the East you are always walking on somebody's
grave, and crackling static from a dying radio filled
the night with rumours of wars fought and yet to be fought,
all that old news, that up-to-the-minute history. Sandbags

and barbed wire divorced the Old and New Jerusalem, and history was a veil the colour of old blood over the valley between. There was music from a wedding;

Fools have always danced too close to the border.

I'm sending these letters to your old address in the New Jerusalem; now there is one Jerusalem, but we know that is an illusion; the whore belongs to no one for any length of time. What is sure is the passage of cats through their easy kingdom. Do you still live there? Are you alive or dead in the awful holy city, killed in the war that declares itself forever? Twenty years have passed and we're still sitting there, Josef, younger and older than death, discussing the endless names of God, Lord of a nameless world, looking out over the valley black with blood, over the vivid darkness of No Man's Land

To the divided city.

ii

What time is it now on the beach at Jaffa?

Remember that Arab boy who knocked my breath out early one morning? He asked me the time and I told him, then he threw me to the ground and crashed to his knees and held me down until my wrists throbbed. I noticed his fine white teeth, and the old houses, deserted and two-dimensional like

studio props against the turquoise backdrop of the sea. The
sun did not shine on those walls – it roared. And the
Mediterranean had a deep pulse

Like the beat of a giant clock.

The beach was crowded with fish-skulls, and how violent
the sun was! We kicked and thrashed and cursed, each in
his own separate tongue. All I did was give him the time
and all Hell broke loose; kids emerged from behind the
walls trailing kites, and surrounded us, cheering. My braids,
my shorts, my naked Anglo-Saxon knees had offended him,
I learned later. Another time, in a village outside of Jerusalem,
I was mistaken for a sabra and stoned by small Arab boys,
so I walked around for weeks with a hole in my head.

How easily one becomes the enemy.

Josef, have you noticed that a thin film has settled over
everything? You peel it away and the world is a raw nerve,
throbbing and throbbing, even the stones are throbbing.
There is nothing but this throbbing, this ancient pulse. If you
see that boy on the beach at Jaffa, tell him the time. It is two
minutes to midnight, though it feels like morning. The first
battle of this war has begun on the beach at Jaffa. All battles
begin on the beach at Jaffa. The sea is booming out the real
hour of the world:

It is countdown; it is the same time everywhere.

iii

Do you still write your angry avant-garde plays?

I have the photo you sent me, of actors with mime-white
faces all dying in different ways. Some go all limp and
funny, they give up their hold on reality; others just die like
clocks, they wind down. You always loved irony; there was
that play about the man in the British army fighting the Nazis,
then in the Irgun fighting the British.

It was the folly, you wrote me, the *foolness* of it all.

We sat all night long and listened to your friends play jazz on
the roof of the theatre where you lived; we discussed how
modern drama differed in the East and West. You said an old
writer had called you a beatnik and tried to rough you up.
Kids down in the streets below us screamed in the lost dialects
of Babylon. I had just seen Kirk Douglas in *Spartacus* speaking
Hebrew. You said – Look at the children, why

Do we keep making the beautiful children?

There was a beggar you tried to befriend, but he screamed
"God will burn you!" when you offered him money or cigarettes.
He had seen his family consumed in a village in Iraq and
they had never stopped burning. In the West, you said,
you hunger for violence; you flirt with it. In the East we have it;

That is the difference.

And years later you write to tell me politics does not matter, only theatre. Night falls like a dead bird or a dusty curtain. Are the kids still screaming in the streets below you? Tell them to stop, tell them all to stop and watch your mime-white clowns dancing down the foolish night, playing live, playing dead, playing everything that is allowed in the theatres of war.

The folly, Josef, the foolness of it all.

iv

This is a story, a letter and a dream.

You go into the desert, looking for the ten lost tribes of your mind. The bus is crammed with laughing sabras, their rifles slung over their shoulders. A Bedouin with a transistor radio under his black robes listens to ambiguous news from Jerusalem. The bus goes into the Negev. In Beersheba your wicked black camera aims itself at an Arab woman and her child. She demands money for whatever part of their souls you intend to steal. She suckles her child, her magnificent dark breast exposed: it is as though the child is suckling the night. She turns away from the camera;

It is her face she wishes to hide.

(You write to tell me you have joined the army because you must. The men are circulating a funny joke about Arabs and hyenas; some Arabs think that hyenas are succubi who

jump on a man's back and suck his brains out so he goes
crazy. In madness he will never enter heaven. The army considers
loosing a pack of hyenas on the Arabs if other weapons
fail. Laughter abounds. The Arabs have turned back in terror,
leaving the desert full of shoes. You and your men, you
add, have pushed on to Sinai, and

You have just dipped your foot in the Suez Canal.)

Here in the desert you go mad; death triggers the madness.
The sand turns to water, to golden snow. The lost tribes
dance in a horrible mirage in front of your eyes. Then
evening falls and black sand veils your skin; the arid night
will suck you in. Death stutters its idiot message in the
throats of the guns. Death has sucked your brains out: no
one will enter heaven now. The hyenas are all laughing at
some sick joke as you leave the desert behind. The bus is
crammed with cameras and radios.

It is just a few minutes to the end of the world.

V

And when it ends, when we finally break the Law—

The stars retreat, the trees fall into fire, the bones of
antelopes are found among the rivers, the waters flow backwards,
the spines of the sea are broken. The universe disowns us;
through forests of missiles.

We come to the Dead, the speechless Sea.

Desert saints died on their knees here; they loved, and their love was a holy wound carved by God who lusted for their bodies and their minds, who claimed and kidnapped them —the thin Essenes, the wise men holier than air. The fire in their souls ignited us and we tried to love, but

Our love was a black love born of sorrow,

An unholy wound we carved in God, a gash in the cosmos where the final void oozed in. Unable to love the smallest things we let fall singing through our hands – lucid animals and birds and flowers – to cherish life after birth, we gave birth to this death.

We announced the coming of a terrible kingdom and it came.

The parched sea drains, the caves give up their dehydrated scrolls, cylindrical coffins of words, parchment auguries. The prophecies are gasps, the dry white sounds of death. Enraged by wounds we cannot heal, and blind with fear which has become as true and usual as breath, we give ourselves over to the lords of death. The Law is broken; we enter

The kingdom. We come to the Dead, the speechless Sea.

vi

Josef, all my letters to you are lies.

In Jerusalem and Tel Aviv and Beirut there are children at
recess wearing many colours, there are beggars with the
world scooped out of their eyes, there are khaki-coloured
walls, Yemenites selling thread, matches, combs, soap, needles,
ribbons; everyone is hammering or cooking or selling
beer and halvah and kebab and falafel. There are pink and
gold walls and everything is full of the sweet conflicting
smells of leather, and bread baking

Thousands of years.

Over Beirut jets send out bright globes of heat to disperse
the missiles, as they dive into the pink and gold morning.
This day escalates into Nuclear Night. Things do not fall
apart; it is worse: everything is fused in an awful centre. The
people of Hiroshima did not have time to die; they melted.
In Jerusalem and Tel Aviv and Beirut the street vendors have
nothing left to sell, and all the colours of the many-coloured
children

Burn into one.

The dead of the earth are masters of the night; they slide
sideways into our dreams. They are the bloated white
corpses of Sabra, fat as larvae, the four hundred bodies floating
years ago down the Mekong River, roped together like
ancestral memories, they are the saints and guerrillas on
wooden crosses, they are the dead of history and the dead of

this moment. I want to say all the dead of the earth sleep in
peace somewhere, their eyelids covered with Roman coins.
But that is not true; that is poetry. The truth is Nuclear
Night, the truth is

Shatila, fat with death, the broken horses.

vii

But there are moments when we dare to believe Peace—

Moments held in the spaces between other moments, like
the blue and red glow in the sections of Chagall's windows
in Jerusalem, moments when the world is in holy communion
with itself. A moment hanging breathlessly over the waters
of Galilee, the sea which is not a sea, the groves along
the shore dark with summer,

The cool, miraculous waves of Kinneret.

A moment in a small hotel with an old man who was a
sheriff in the Wild East, talking of Lawrence and Palestine,
and the radio tells us a new satellite has been launched at
Cape Canaveral. He is almost deaf, so I point to the dark
skies above Galilee and make circles with my hand. All the
wars he has fought

Retreat into the silence of space.

A moment reading Engel's *Dialectics of Nature* in a small
room in Jerusalem. "The dialectical immutability of matter...

it can neither be created nor destroyed." In my mind, the Koran echoing: "The eternal God; He begetteth not; neither is He begotten."

A moment in late afternoon in mystic Safed,

When the passionate light shines on purple grapes, yellow beer, the green and violet slopes of Mount Miron. Giant insects with golden shells walk through my room and the pale-faced Hassidim, God dancing in their heads, talk quietly in the streets. And through it all, Chagall's mules and donkeys with velvet eyes wander around everywhere. All these moments, and the sun blasting the windows in Jerusalem.

Breaking the glass into perfect nuclei of light.

viii

History is wearing then, Josef; soon there may be no more history.

This comes back to me: I told you how I joined a religious group on Mount Zion and we went into the Room of the Last Supper and fell on our knees and I prayed and then rose to an epidemic of cameras. Everybody photographing each other saying cheese in front of the ancient pillars and walls. I wondered how the pictures turned out; I never saw them. The priest kept reminding us that This Place Is Holy, and signs said:

The Enemy Is Watching You.

Eyes stared at us through binoculars; Israeli soldiers threw cigarettes to the Arab sentries; they were close enough to spit from one side of the border to the other. But you go any closer and you get your head blown off, we were told, because The Enemy Is Watching You. Which enemy, I asked you, Josef— the sentries, the Antichrist, Moloch, or

Our true selves, trapped in the undeveloped film?

I have your last letter in front of me now. You write: "Something very funny happened. Now this moment when I'm sitting and writing you, remembering our walk near the walls of the Old City, suddenly the Arabs begin to shoot. From my window I see that it's going to be a big fight— bombs, guns and all the rest of it. You see it's very interesting here in our Bloody Holy Land.

With the name of Jerusalem, Youssy."

That place where you live is not a city but a meaning; it is the conscience of the world. You cannot destroy her or forget her, you told me, she will make you return. Now I look back and see her stretched out like a gold spider over the hills of Judah; the walls of the Old City melt and sizzle in the distance. Perhaps it is not there at all.

From my window I see that it's going to be a big fight.

Will you write me back? *We are still young, and everything is a moment away from being destroyed.* Do you still live up there on the roof of the old theatre? *Lord, lead us out of this impossible night.* Do you still take walks through the graveyard where we sat? Twenty years have passed and we're still sitting there, Josef, younger and older than death, looking out over the ____ darkness of No Man's Land

In the divided city.

Manitou Poem

"To enter this world was to step into, not out of, the real world."
—SELWYN DEWDNEY, *The Sacred Scrolls of the Southern Ojibway*

So I must stand away from the stone to enter the stone,
To dream the idea of the stone, the stone which is all stones,
        the first and final stone,
Its source being, its Manitou.

As in puberty I dreamed my lifelong protector, who showed me
How to navigate impossible rivers, who made me as the world's
        first person, breathing
Fire and poetry.

The strangers who divided the world into good and evil were wrong.
The Great Lynx Misshipeshu who dwells beneath ambivalent water
        is both benevolent
Lord, and devil.

And I am become the powerful dreamer who dreams his way through
To reality, to enter and ignite the stone, to illumine
        from within
Its perfect paradox, its name.

Grey Owl's Poem

There is no chart of his movement through the borrowed forest,
A place so alien that all he could do with it
          was pretend it was his own
And turn himself into an Indian, savage and lean,
A hunter of the forest's excellent green secret.

For all his movements through the forest were
In search of himself, in search of Archie Belaney,
          a lone predator in London
Telling the very king: *I come in peace, brother.*
(The princess thinking how alien he was, how fine.)

Stranger and stranger to return to the forest
With the beavers all laughing at him, baring
          their crazy orange teeth
And the savage secret – if there ever was one –
Never revealed to him. Stranger and stranger to return to

The female forest, the fickle wind erasing his tracks,
The receding treeline, and the snowbanks moving and moving.

The Name of the Night

The name of the night our mouths nibbling
the dark bread of love the dark flowers of love

The name of the night birds flying in all directions
dropping crumbs and petals on the world

The name of the night our mouths drinking
the dark wine of death the dark blood of death

The name of the night our bodies falling
a rain of wine and blood at midnight falling

The name of the night the black mouth of Africa
the open cavernous mouth of Africa

The gaping bird mouths of the dead of Africa
mute roar of the dark children across the land

Seeing Eye Dogs

for Barbara

If my cat sits long enough on my typewriter
She might write something wonderful.

Meanwhile the dog stars, the sundogs, those fake suns
Blind us who are addicted to light and dark, whose eyes
Are windows often peering into nowhere,
Into the phony houses of our lives,

While you and your black all-seeing dog
Lying in the corner of your room deflect me
From the gates of hell, then he
Leads you through the streets of this shady city.

Already I perceive the holes in my vision, the blind spots
I dare not face, I and my fellow fools
Glancing through day and night, dancing, adoring
The glare of our darkness.

Last night on TV Sherlock Holmes got into a carriage
Led by a horse with blinkers, and Sherlock's eyes
Went prancing, reflecting clues and theories
And focusing, finally, on the fact (surmise)
That the world was just as mad as he was.

And went home and shot up on something from the boredom
The boredom of it all.

Then I watched this fish with the craziest camouflage ever—
A phony eye at his tail so his enemies couldn't tell
If he was coming or going or what the hell
He thought he was doing.

So when I turn away from you I have eyes at the back of my head
Which allow me to see a world I've left behind—
And the dear creature who is your eyes
Lies regarding me with horror and surprise,
That I might glimpse reality perhaps once in a lifetime,

Or if my cat sits long enough on my typewriter
She might write something wonderful, sublime.

Fireworks

In memory of Marian Engel

A year after your death, in the spleen of winter
Part of your garden lies buried in my garden
Where I transplanted it. I wonder
Where you are now— (it isn't exactly heaven
because you said once you knew all about heaven
and didn't want to go there). Nevertheless
As I celebrate your life I celebrate your entry
Into some unconditional kingdom.

Friend, let your death be fireworks
Like the pinwheels and burning schoolhouses
(we have so much to unlearn)
You had in your garden on the 24th of May
A hundred years ago when we were less than young.

Let it be a conflagration, a sign,
Like all those loud outspoken flowers
Which will burn all summer in my back yard—
(the Japanese lanterns, bright audacious orange
against the garden wall)—

Everything struggling to become what it already is
And we who are left behind you
Struggling to become what we already are.

Winter 1986

In the Garden of the Chelsea Arts Club

Alastair the poet tells me *nothing dies,*
    and in his eyes the great trouble of love
As he leads me through the garden gate
    where sunflowers grow tall as towers,
Past a little statue and a pool much gazed upon
    by Augusta John and others, sits down
And takes a nap and leaves me alone
    in the outrageous garden.

But endless time is the enemy, I thought,
    and suddenly at the far end of the garden
I locate the enemy in the form of the resident tortoise
    who is moving toward me sickeningly slowly.
Under the shell of the tortoise is the dark spirit
    of the garden, a naked thing
Devoid of anything, even hunger; it has not eaten
    for a hundred years
And still it is alive; it eats my eyes.

And Alastair who is 92 told me *nothing dies.*

The tortoise stares at a white petal with ferocious hatred;
    he cares for nothing but himself,
The world offends him, he is hideously sane,
    he has been in the garden
Since the beginning of time, and will be here forever,
    staring at nothing, staring at everything,
Blind.

But another white petal falls on his back from the tree
    and its weight is enough to kill him.
So beauty is your enemy, I discover, *you* will *die!*
    I leave the ridiculous, gorgeous, unreal garden
With the pool and the tortoise and the ghosts
    of Augustus John and others
And Alastair the poet, his eyelids slowing opening,
    eyes following me, eyes which will never really
Close.

London, 1984

Languages (2)

When we were fifteen my girlfriend and I used to sit in the back seats of Dundas Street streetcars and whip out our vio lins and play Bach's *Concerto for Violins in D Minor* all the way to Yonge Street. This was to startle people and make them notice us. Then we walked barefoot all over downtown before it became a fad in the Sixties, also to startle people and make them notice us. Some of these things worked, but the one thing that never worked was when we sat in the back seats of streetcars and spoke loudly in a language we made up on the spur of the moment, syllable by syllable. We didn't realize that in this country one more language, especially one more unofficial language would do you no good at all, although knowing only one language of any kind in this country would also do you no good; you had to know more than one to survive. All those mangled feet, all those wounded alphabets, all those illicit violins.

Sunday Morning Sermon

The cat sits on the fence, turning into a bird, turning into a river, turning into an antelope. In the beginning the world was the sweet heart of nowhere; then everything became very articulate, which was marvellous considering nothing had a name. The lush exotic Nothing was crammed with forms and the forms were Something. Flowers brushed your legs, pleading with you to love them. They were red— no, red was the sound they made; actually they were blue and yellow. Now you can see as much as you choose; you can watch that tree as it sits there doing nothing, or watch that tree as it zooms through space. But if you think you are starting to know anything at all— beware. The cat has more surprises.

Barker Fairly and the Blizzard

It was freezing and wet and everybody was being blown all over the street and taking shelter whenever they could, when Barker emerged from the swirling cloud of the blizzard, walking slowly and thoughtfully, his cap at a superb angle. It was a few years ago, so he couldn't have been much more thank ninety. *Gwendolyn,* he said, as the gale pushed me sideways and I crashed into a wall, *I've been thinking about suffering. Does the artist have to suffer, do you think? Yes,* I said. *Definitely. The older I get the more I suffer so it must be necessary. And furthermore it is packed with meaning.* Barker looked at me quietly as several people held onto each other's waists with the man in front attached to a telephone pole, to avoid being blown away. *I don't think so, I really don't think so,* he said, as two women and a man were washed into the gutter. *We're here to bring joy; we weren't meant to suffer at all.* And he leaned into the exquisite storm and was gone.

Past and Future Ghosts

Everything is already known, but we proceed as though we know nothing. I have lived in houses haunted by ghosts from the future as well as the past— ghosts of my future and past selves as well as ghosts of others. It's very simple; we all just move from room to room in these time-houses and catch glimpses of one another in passing. As a child in one house I used to see this older woman who was myself grown up, and thirty years later I went back there and met the child, who was waiting for me to come. Who is haunting whom? Right now some future ghosts are re-decorating the house I live in; I see them out of the corner of my eye, tearing down certain walls and inventing new ones. Look out – you who inhabit those rooms of my future – I'm coming after you. I'm starting to haunt you, I'm starting right now.

The Transparent Womb

Here's why I never had a child. Because down the lane
behind the Morgentaler clinic the mother of a tribe of alley
cats nudges towards me the one she knows will die after its
first and last drink of warm water in the depths of winter,
because the bag lady down the street (who was once a child)
tells me she won't go on welfare because that's only for people
who are really hard up, because I collect kids and cats
and strangers (or they collect me), and at Halloween the poor
kids come shelling out and one boy wears a garbage bag
over his head with holes cut out for eyes and says does it
matter what he's supposed to *be*, and his sister wears the
same oversize dress she wears every day because it's already
a funny, horrible costume, hem flopping around her ankles,
the eternal hand-me-down *haute mode* of the poor, because

They wander into my house all the time asking "got any
fruit?" because their parents spend their welfare cheques on
beer and pork and beans and Kraft Dinner and more beer,
they won't eat vegetables with funny names like the Greeks
and the Wops, so the kids are fat, poor fat, fat with starch
and sugar, toy food, because

The kids in Belfast in that news photo were trying to pull a
gun away from a British soldier in a terrible tug of war
where nobody won, and

My foster kid in El Salvador is called Jesus.

Here's why I never had a child: Because they're so valuable I could never afford one, because I never thought it was a good way to glue a man to me, because I never thought I had to prove *I* could do it while they're starving everywhere and floating in gutters and screaming with hunger. All this in our time. All the world's children are ours, all of them are already mine.

The Man with Three Violins

Or you think there are three violins because there are three black cases strapped over his shoulder. You see him all the time on Bloor Street; he's carrying them somewhere, he's always been carrying them somewhere, years now. (Cats and dogs love him because animals love poets and musicians and anyone who breaks the law.) The truth is that if you opened the three cases you'd find in the first case: pages of thumb-prints of famous chess players, a collection of ancient Persian knives, authentic relics of the true cross, and little bottles of water from the Nile and the Thames and the St. Lawrence, and in the second case: Peruvian salt and pepper sets, cedarwood camels carved in Yemen, international stamps, so many you could mail anything from anywhere to anywhere, pebbles from Troy and the Parthenon, a napkin signed by Gregory Peck, and a scroll from Tibet. The third case is empty. Like his eyes. Full of lonely. An archive of nothing. There are no violins.

You Know Me

I promise I will never stop you in the middle
of the street and say: Here I am

I am she who has invaded your dreams
I am she who you secretly adore

I promise I will never identify myself in any
obvious way; I will never embarrass you in public

But you know me, sir, and you know that I know
that you know that I know that you know me

My God, the nights we have spent together
my God, the times we have come together

Each one of us alone, in the unblind darkness

Beloved.

Absences

You have never looked so fine
as now, when you are not here.

—So shot with light,
so sharply defined—

I cut my finger on the white
edges
of this paper.
I cut my eyes on the keen edges of your
absences.

I am faithless to you, distant one.
I lie with your blinding shadow, your

White mind.

The Timing

Some days I cannot look at you,
I am dizzy with wisdom, I am struck dumb. Stars
Are fossils in space, the clocks of the city
Wind down. I tell all my poems to go home.

You slide through the slits of these minutes,
The slim air sliced by your presence, your perfect
Timing.

Help. I am numb with your beauty, I am
Besieged by truth.
Your hands are as lean as the long hours
Before midnight. Time
Is speechless as it strikes your mouth.

These preposterous lines proceed no further.

A Stillness of Waiting

"the stillness which I particularly associate with the Egyptians, a stillness of waiting, not of death."

– Henry Moore

How I long to return to you,
to enter the bright world of our youth.

I wear rings on the upper joints of my fingers
like those ladies from Pompeii. I wear
the red and blue and gold of Ur,
I wear the brutal jewels of Babylon.

The years crawl by like scorpions.

In the dusk and in the long shadows of the past I was
beneath your ribs, I was
between your legs, I was
inside your mind.

How I long to feel the dark voyage
of your hand along my spine.

How I long to return to you,
to enter the dark world of your mouth.

How I long for you my brother, my soul.

Daynights

I don't trust you for a single second, but
My bones turn gold in your hands' warm holding
In the dark or in the bright heart of the morning,

And suddenly the days are longer than anything,
Longer than Tolstoy, longer than Proust, longer
Than anything.

But the days are also diving into night, and

I told you our end lay in our beginning
So we drink to our end, always remembering
That at the bottom of the goblets of Pompeii
Was the skull; we crawl

Out of the night utterly broken, bruises
All over our souls,

But this pain returns me to the world.

Even in the end your perfidy serves me, so
The cry we made when we came, love,
Will sound the same and is the same
As the cry we will make when we go.

November

If you knew that I would lie here on this dark November morn
Considering nothing but your eyes, your eyes,
Would you laugh with disbelief, surprise,
Remembering how we spoke of calculus and stars
And ruined civilizations and world powers
And their stupid chess games and unwon wars?

And how the innocence of this land may lie
Not in what we think is weakness, but in strength—
(What would they have called us if they thought
They'd found China instead of India—
Mandarins, Mongols, Chinks?)

And how at the end of the evening, Celestial
Tea was served, and I looked into your eyes, your eyes
And considered abandoning politics and poetry
For the dark spirits and spices of your body,
As subtle and alien and intimate and known to me
As you are, who are able
As all multiple and perfect equations are
To bend and break my mind?

I loved you. So sue me. A dozen stars
Went nova. Just like that.

The Lion

for Robert Duncan

To love is to be remarkable, and flawless.
It is to wear the yellow crown of a flawless beast
Forever.

It is to inhabit the flawless and exceeding universe
Forever.

It is to summon the wonderful numbers
Which add up to the mighty stars.
It is learning to divide and multiply by these numbers.

I swear by all the famous, ancient lions I have known
That the mighty children yet to come
Will foster finer stars,

For they are the true lords, born of morning
Whose coming will call us down
Like a deck of cards.

To love is to be remarkable, and flawless.
It is to wear the yellow crowns
Of all the gods.

Marino Marini's Horses & Riders

So we embrace our end in our beginning.

All we have to give each other is
Our breath, our darkness breathing
Life into the dying lungs of the night.

Enter my darkness, I give you
My darkness;
Together for one second we are light.

We proceed in beautiful devastating stages
Towards our end, as the horse and rider
Collapse together in the catastrophe of love.

I lie in the night of your breath.
There is only your breath, all else has gone.

The horse dissolves between the rider's thighs,
The world dissolves before the rider's eyes.

So now, in the animal darkness, come.

A Coin for the Ferryman

In this rain that lasts forever
I embrace a loneliness like no other
And live with it till it becomes my friend
And cast this savage poem upon the waters.

My love, I could not save you from your life
Nor you from mine, but I promise you these lines
Are as real as our names, as the pain we know
Of our coming and going, our swimming, our drowning.

The afterworld is the preworld, is this world,
Is the dawning when you are drawn taut as a bowstring
Or detached as a drawbridge, or are indeed
As liquid and lyric as a spear cast into water.

So I cast this ancient coin upon the waters
(Whose currency is long since cancelled)—
An offering to Charos who knows all too well
Of our coming and going, our swimming, our drowning

And will lead us both across the final waters.

The Tao of Physics

In the vast spaces of the subatomic world where
Matter has a tendency to exist
The lord of Life is breathing in and out,
Creating and destroying the universe
With each wave of his breath.

And my lord Siva dances in the city streets,
His body a fierce illusion of flesh, of energy,
The particles of light cast off from his hair
Invade the mighty night, the relative night, this dream.

Here where events have a tendency to occur
My chair and all its myriad inner worlds
Whirl around in the carousel of space; I hurl
Breathless poems against my lord Death, send these
Words, these words
Careening into the beautiful darkness.

THE BIRDS

1993

THE BIRDS

after the play by Aristophanes

CHARACTERS

†

Y: A young black man, citizen of the *Metropolis*

X: A young white man, citizen of the *Metropolis*

SERVANT OF EPOPS: a bird

EPOPS: Half man, half bird

LEADER: An owl
POET
SEER
SURVEYOR
PEKING DUCK
GODDESS
PROMETHEUS
POSEIDON
HERACLES

VARIOUS BIRDS

†

In order of their appearance
SERVANT OF EPOPS
EPOPS
CUCKOO CLOCK
WEATHERVANE
ALARM CLOCK
PLASTIC BIRD
LE CROISSANT
LA CREPE
HORNED GRUNCHEON
PURPLE-TAILED TERROR
RECITING BIRD
RED-FOOTED MADCAP
SCARLET PIMPERNEL
KISSING QUILL
SHAMELESS HUSSY
STAR-SPANGLED BANNER
TWO-IN-THE-BUSH
LEADER
PEKING DUCK

Y

(Going to stage front to address audience) This is it, then. We've done all we can. Rotten luck. We're lost. This place is Nowhere... I mean, *West* of Nowhere, East of Somewhere... I mean... well, maybe I should explain— *(he crouches down and chews on a piece of grass, looking up now and again at the audience)* My friend and I, you see, are slightly mad. Just slightly. We're trying to find a kind of Utopia, you know, an *ideal* place to live. The perfect setting, conducive to human happiness, health and spiritual well-being. We checked out everything—everything in the *Metropolis*, that is: high-rises, low-rises, flats over stores with the traffic outside driving you mad. Lonely rooms that inspire you to do nothing except play games like Monopoly and Solitaire. Everywhere the noise, the insane rush, the pushing and shoving... the nightmare which we called 'civilization'... the *Metropolis...*

X

(Getting up and joining Y at front of stage) Most people would give *anything* for the chance to become citizens of the *Metropolis.* Wouldn't you? But my friend and I, who were born there, are simply dying to get away from it! We don't *hate* the place, but—

Y

The *Metropolis* is a fine place, a lovely place, but—

X

(Screaming in spite of himself) Housing shortages. Inflation. Sky-high rents. Insane taxes. Taxes on everything from your inflatable wings to your *crutches. (To his bird)* What do think, friend? Could you sublet your *bird-cage* to me for a month or two? Eh? What about the West Wing? No? The East?

Y

(Muttering to himself) Wage controls, price freezes… the cryptic language of a civilization which has gone only *partially* mad. The rest will follow. We will not be there. We will not be there when the *Metropolis* devours itself. It's enough to drive you *nuts.*

X

It's a nice place to visit, but who wants to live there? *(He puts his head between his knees and sobs)*

Y

(Patting X on the back) That's why we've left. We're going to find a nice place, a super-nice place, an *impossibly* nice place to live in. *(Addressing the audience)* You see… my friend and I *are* slightly mad… *(Pauses)* But we won't settle for anything less than the best. Right? *(He shakes X to restore him to normal)* Right, friend? Right?

X

Absolutely right. *(Addressing audience)* We were told to find *Epops* and consult him on the matter. These birds we have are supposed to lead us to him, to *Epops.* Epops is a sort of a bird who used to be a man, but that's a long story. Anyway, if we can *find* this Epops, he's bound to know something. He's been all over everywhere. I mean— he's been *around.* He's flown all over the planet, he must have seen *something.*

Y

Down with the Metropolis, down with civilization.

X

Up with anarchy. The bird of freedom is on the wing. The wind is on the bird… I mean… *(Faltering)* Where *are we*? *(The crow begins to caw loudly)* Hey, come here. The crow's trying to tell me something. *(Y moves towards him, and the blue jay also squawks. X and Y are drawn towards a large rock situated in front of the thorny bush)*

Y

We must be getting warm, brother. There are *birds* around here somewhere. We gotta make some kind of noise to stir them up.

X

Why don't you kick the rock, friend?

Y

Why don't you bash your head on it, *friend*— it's thicker.

X

O shut up. Let's get a stone. We can bang on it with a stone...

Y

A *sound* idea. *(He finds a stone, and he and X bang on the rock alternately)*

X

Hello there... anybody home?

Y

Anybody there?

X

Let's trying calling Epops— you know, *Epops.* He's been around, he's our connection. He's bound to get us *somewhere.*

Y

Hello there. You in the stone. Come in. Come in. Epops, Epops? Calling Epops— do you read? Epops? Over and out. Well, that's that. *(X and Y stare at one another in despair, until there is a commotion in the bush. The SERVANT of EPOPS charges out of the bush. He is a horrifying sight, with huge feathers and a crown of fiery red maple leaves)*

SERVANT

(Shrieking hysterically) You rang? *Pourquoi?* What do you want? And why? (*X and Y clutch each other in fear)*

Y

Look at that beak, man. He's ferocious, he's *wild.*

X

T-t-t-take us to your *leader.*

Y

Exactly. You took the words out of my mouth. T-t-take us to your leader.

SERVANT

C'est impossible. Il dormi.

X

(Whispering to Y) It's impossible. He's sleeping…

Y

He's *sleeping?*

SERVANT

Oui. And furthermore, he's *out.* Ha. *Il n'est pas ici.*

Y

(Whispering in X's ear) Ask him, I mean, *ask him.* If his *pen* is on the *table…*

X

(Whispering) If *whose* pen is on *whose* table?

Y

If his *aunt's* pen is on *her* table?

X

Why?

SERVANT

(Doing a little dance) He is out. He is in. He is sleeping. He is swimming. His pen is on the table... They have not found the *plume* of his *tante,* nor have they found the *table* of his *oncle...*

X

O shut up. Shut *up.* Look, can't my friend and I just introduce ourselves...?

SERVANT

You're bird-catchers, aren't you? You don't have to tell me, I simply *know. (Screaming in a high falsetto)* Well in that case, you're doomed, utterly *doomed.*

Y

No, no— we're not bird-catchers. We're not even *men*, really I mean—

SERVANT

What *are* you, then?

Y

(Stuttering) I'm a Fearless, which, as you probably know, is a rare African bird which used to live in a constant state of panic and terror and ate nothing but ju-jubes. Now, of course, times have changed, and—

SERVANT

Never mind all that. *(To X)* Who are *you*?

X

Wouldn't it be appropriate at this point for us to ask who *you* are?

SERVANT

(Obviously pleased at the question and the chance it gives him to elaborate on himself) I? Oh, I see what you mean... you mean

me. Oh, I don't know. Let's see, then. Who *am* I? Who *am* I? *(Pacing up and down dramatically and putting on ridiculous airs)* Does anyone really *know* who he, she or it, in fact is? I suppose you might say I'm a slave-bird. Or at least, a glorified servant-bird. Or something. When my master (who as you know, used to be a man) was turned into a half man, half bird, he begged me to become a bird, too, so I could continue to serve him. *C'est la vie,* I said to myself...

Y

(Whispering to X) He's doing that French thing again. Ask him if the *pen's* on the *table*...

X

Sssh.

SERVANT

... and I decided that was the only course of action open to me. So I became a bird. And now... life's a breeze. If he feels like sardines on toast, I head for the sea. If he fancies Vichysoisse, I grab a pot and hightail it to wherever I can find leeks and potatoes. If he's into *soufflés,* I...

Y

Enough. Do us a favour, and just *call* your master.

SERVANT

Can't. No kidding. He's sound asleep. He stuffed himself with berries and a side-dish of creamed worm. I mean, of course, *vers à la crème.* Sounds better in a foreign tongue, you know. Some things *do.*

X

Oh look, we're getting nowhere. Wake him up anyway. Please, *please.*

SERVANT

(Retreating into the bush) All right, but he'll be furious, I warn you. *(The SERVANT disappears into the bush. In the interim, X and Y release their birds at stage right, over the Sheer Drop)*

EPOPS

(Calling from within the bush) Let me out. Untangle this bush at once. Do something. This is so *undignified.* Why do I have to emerge from this stupid *bush. (Amid much commotion, EPOPS emerges from the bush, covered with leaves and twigs. Skinny and ridiculous, he is half man, half bird. He wears a large headdress with three floppy crests— red, white and blue… stars, fleurs de lis, maple leaves, etc. He wears a punctured pillow under his clothes, so that whenever he moves, he sends up clouds of floating feathers)*

Y

(Whistling) Will you look at this. Look at those crazy things on his head, friend. Who is this guy— a walking flag? Or…"is it a bird, is it a plane, is it…"

EPOPS

(In slightly nasal tones) You wanted to see me? *(X and Y slowly circle around EOPS, nodding their heads in pity)*

X

Someone's given you a rough time, eh?

Y

Pity, pity, pity.

EPOPS

Are you making fun of me? I was once a *man,* you know.

X

And now…?

EPOPS

Now, I'm essentially a *bird,* you idiot. Anyone can see that.

Y

What's wrong with your feathers?

EPOPS

Well, some of them are falling off here and there…

X

What's the matter? Are you sick?

EPOPS

No, I'm *moulting,* you fool. All birds *moult.* Look. *(Jumping up and down sending more feathers flying)* Birds moult. I moult. Therefore, I am a bird.

Y

I'll buy that. That's philosophically sound.

EPOPS

Who are *you*?

X

We're men.

EPOPS

Extraordinary. *Both* of you? How marvellous. Where are your from?

X

The place where they have all those large grey buildings. The place that they call *civilization*. The *Metropolis*.

EPOPS

(After a long pause) Are you officials?

X

God no. if anything, we're anti-officials.

EPOPS

(Sitting on the ground and attempting to brush off his loose feathers) What brings you here?

Y

We came to consult you.

EPOPS

Me? You're not serious? Me, why me? *(Half-laughing and half-weeping)* You're kidding.

Y

(Sitting down beside EPOPS and helping him brush away the feathers) Look, you used to be a man like us, right? And like us, you had piles of debts which you couldn't possibly *pay.* You know… debts which present themselves in the forms of dollars or of dreams… debts that eventually detract from the *soul,* or at the very least, the *character. Debits,* I might say. The opposite of *credits…*

X

(Approaching) Why has he suddenly gone green? Fan him, fan him. *(X and Y fan EPOPS with their hands)*

Y

What I *wanted* to say was… when you turned into a bird, you got to see all kinds of lands and seas from a *bird's-eye view*—right? You got to see things from the *air*. That means you've got human knowledge *plus* bird knowledge. See what I mean? That's what we need. *You* can point us in the *right direction*. You can suggest the possible Utopias. You're the one who *flies*, man…

EPOPS

(Pondering) Mmmm… are you looking for something *larger* than the *Metropolis*? Larger and classier, perhaps? More cosmopolitan? More… mmm… *fun*?

Y

Just nicer, man. *Nicer*.

EPOPS

You mean something more… mmm… *gentile, refined?*

X

Something nice. Something human, something real, something *ideal*. A city where you can spread your wings and *fly*.

Y

I like that. "Spread your wings and fly…!" Oh, I like that.

X

Yeh. A place where your neighbours are your *friends*, no questions asked. Where you don't have to build fences between your property and another guy's. Where you share the wealth and nobody goes without. Where you can have a crazy party every night if you feel like it— for no reason at all…

Y

A place where you can spread your wings and *fly*. And chicks, beautiful chicks all over the place with these crazy fathers who actually *want* you to make out with their gorgeous daughters! Crazy fathers who'd be insulted if you *didn't*. Wow.

EPOPS

Well… Mmmm… I've been around a *lot*, but—

X

You must have seen something! I mean you're a bird. Well, almost.

EPOPS

I haven't done all that much flying lately, but— let me think. *(He chews idly on one of his fallen feathers, like a large quill pen, until he sneezes and casts it away)* A-ha! I have it. Paris.

X

Forget it. I've heard they speak a foreign tongue there.

EPOPS

London?

Y

I've heard they speak a foreign tongue there.

EPOPS

Rome?

X

They speak a foreign tongue there.

EPOPS

Maybe you should just stay where you are. Mmmm… or if you don't like it *here*, then split. Oh, I don't know… *(He shrugs, and sends up more feathers)* Why did you come to me, anyway? I'm not a magician. *(X and Y turn away dejectedly)*

Y

It almost makes you wonder, doesn't it?…that this whole idea of Utopia is *strictly* for the birds.

X

You said it, friend. *(They pace up and down for a couple of moments until they stop dead in their tracks, and stare at each other with 'Eureka' written all over their faces)*

X

What *did* you say?

Y

I said—

X

That's what I *thought* you said.

EPOPS

(Getting up in a cloud of feathers) My God. *Mon Dieu.* You're *right. (Becoming doubtful again and sinking back into a sitting position)* At least I think you are. That is... Mmmm... let's see... *(X and Y pounce on EPOPS)*

X

Come on, tell us, tell us, tell us.

Y

Tell us, tell us, tell us... *what's it like to live among the birds? (Half a dozen or so 'flamingos' who form a chorus line in the Can-Can style, enter stage left and breeze out at stage right, over the 'Sheer Drop' sign)*

CHORUS LINE

(Singing) Tell us, tell us, tell us, tell us, Tell us, tell us, tell us, tell us— What's it like to live among the birds...?

EPOPS

What was that? Who were they? Oh well, let's see. Mmmm… what's it like to live among the birds? Hmmm. *(He shrugs)* Well, for one thing… you don't have to carry a wallet!

X

That rules out pick-pockets. But—

EPOPS

Think man, think. If you don't have to carry a wallet, then you don't have to carry all those cards that tell the world who you are, or who you're *supposed* to be.

CHORUS LINE

(Re-entering stage right and exiting stage left) Tell us, Tell us, tell us, tell us, Tell us, tell us, tell us, tell us— What's it like to live among the birds…?

EPOPS

Who *are* those creatures? *(Shrugging)* Well, anyway— let's see. What's it like to live among the birds? Mmmm… your *food* is pretty well taken care of. The gardens are full of eggplants and *exquisite* berries… not to mention poppies, mint, parsley, sage, rosemary and thyme… *(He pauses and remembers the song*

"Marlboro Fair," which he sings) Parsley, sage, rosemary and thyme. Remember me to one who lives there. She once was a true love of mine... *(Remembering himself)* That was, of course, *à propos* of nothing. Hmmm... what was I saying anyway?

X

You were telling us about the availability of food if one is living among the birds.

EPOPS

Exactly. I was just testing your powers of recall. Well, there's just about anything you could ever want in the fields and gardens of the world... *(Picking a few twigs from the nearby bush and chewing on them)* For full-course meals, for feasting, or snacking, or whatever. Not to mention stuff for powerful *herbal remedies...* your valerian, your skullcap, your burdock, your moose-jaw, your worm-wart, your slippery elm bark, your dragon's blood, your squaw root, your flin-flon, your... *(His voice fades away; he seems dazed, or high. He examines the twigs he's been chewing on)* I wonder what that stuff was?... I haven't tried that bush before. It's pretty... powerful... *(He keels over and lies flat on his back)*

Y

(Rushing over to X and grabbing his shoulders in excitement) A fabulous idea is sprouting in my head, friend. Listen to this. Are you ready? We could actually make the birds the *masters of the world. (There is a long pause. X Stares at Y, horrified)*

X

You're off your rock. You've flown your coop. Birdbrain.

Y

No, you're wrong. Listen to me. I've got a vision. I see, I see—*a city*.

EPOPS

(Slowly coming out of his stupor) A city? Where, where?

Y

(Assuming the commanding stance of a Columbus, and pointing towards the Sheer Drop sign) Yonder.

X

That sign says Sheer Drop. That's what it says. It doesn't say 'City.'

EPOPS

(To X, in a loud whisper) I think he's building castles in the air. What do you think?

Y

Come on. I'll show you what I mean.

(X and EPOPS follow him to the Sheer Drop sign)

Y

It's obvious. It's staring us in the face. *(To EPOPS)* Look down, down over the rocks...

EPOPS

Allright, I'm looking down.

Y

Now look up. Straight up.

EPOPS

Allright, I'm looking straight up.

Y

Now turn your head around in circles.

EPOPS

I am. Oh, my neck, my neck.

Y

Now, tell me— *what have you seen?*

EPOPS

Nothing. Everything. Clouds and sky. Sky and clouds. Cloudy skies. The forecast is semi-overcast skies with intermittent showers ending sometime this afternoon. Or, showers interrupted by intermittent patches of blue… however you take your weather… *(Drowsily)*… one thing you can always count on— there'll always be weather…

Y

(Despondently) You didn't see my vision. You didn't see the City.

X

(Gazing out over the Sheer Drop sign) Do you mean… all that out there? All that sky, and all that air, all that *space*? That's bird country, friend… the domain of our fine feathered friends. Layers of air between earth and heaven. I don't see your vision. I don't see any City…

Y

(Muttering to himself) We could lay siege to their needs, their highest ideals. We could starve them out…

X

Who?

Y

The rest of the world, that's who. And even the gods, the false, uncompromising gods…

(Something in his tone makes the other two take notice)

EPOPS

(Slowly) Tell me about your vision… I'm all ears…

X

Come on… what have you seen?

(EPOPS and X position themselves and await Y's answer)

Y

Look— the *air* is between heaven and earth, right? I mean, the air is a sort of buffer zone between what we call 'the gods' and what we call 'man'. OK. *(Pausing)* Now, when we want to go somewhere— that is, *horizontally*— we have to get a thing called a *visa,* right? *(Looking intensely at the other two and pausing for effect)* Well, what if somebody wants to go straight up, or straight down? Who controls that buffer zone between heaven and earth? Who is in a position to issue visas to the envoys from the gods to men?

EPOPS

(Considering for a moment) Why— the birds, of course.

X

Right on. The birds.

Y

The *birds.*

EPOPS

I love it. *Les oiseaux. Les oiseaux. (Stopping, as seized by a dreadful thought)* Wait a minute. I'm not sure that I like this. How does it *work?*

Y

Look at you… you're all in a flutter. *Listen*— it works like this: when men sacrifice to the gods – (whichever gods) – the smoke from their sacrifices travels *upwards.* If you control the air, let's say— then you demand a sort of tribute for allowing the smoke to pass through your territory. Got that? No, you haven't got it. OK, listen. If the aforesaid tribute, or tax, or whatever is *not* paid— then you exercise your absolute rights and *refuse to permit the smoke to pass through.* Without the smoke from the sacrifices, the gods will starve. Now do you get it?

X

I'm starting to. And then what happens…?

Y

Easy. The gods give in.

X

Just like that?

Y

Just like that. And the birds become the masters of the world, the heavens, everything…

“SCRAPBOOK”

Children at Malibar Cottage, Lake Simcoe, study by Alick McEwen. Gwendolyn is on the far right.

RELATED READING
QUESTIONS FOR DISCUSSION AND ESSAYS
RELATED URLs

Westward Ho! *Yearbook*

Gwendolyn was the Literary Editor, and won the school's Literary Contests in 1958 and 1959

Note that at this time she was "McEwen"

Literary Editor
GWEN McEWEN

WESTWARD HO!

WESTERN
TECHNICAL
COMMERCIAL

1958

Toronto
Oct/17

Dear Dad,

Since it's rather hard to keep in touch with one another, I thought it a good idea to drop a line here and there.

First of all, I have some wonderful news I'm sure you'll be delighted to hear. I am going to recieve a cheque for $100 at the Commencement service this year at school! It is, of course, to further my education, and also the percent I got last year was an important factor. I am really thrilled - it makes me feel that my work and interest in school aren't in vain now that I've accomplished something! I'm beginning to realize that I really have the ability to go ahead and achieve an education which seems to be becoming more important to me all the time.

Gwendolyn with her father, 1958 or 1959

Winners of Westward Ho! Literary Contest

GRADE 12 — Story 1 — Gwen McEwen, M 12 G
2 — Pat Baker, C 12 H 1
3 — Marian Hordelski, HE 12 B
Article 1 — Gwen McEwen, M 12 G
2 — Rose Marko, C 12 R1
3 — Don Fuller, C 10 M
Poem 1 — Gwen McEwen, M 12 G
2 — Donna Lee Reid, C 12 A
3 — Nancy Clarke, C 12 M

GRADE 11 — Story 1 — E. Stimpson, C 11 F
2 — Kris Hersymik, Art 11
3 — Thelma Cuddy, C 11 H 1
Article 1 — Michael Frank, M 11 A
2 — Sandra Gough, C 11 H 2 R 2
3 — Jim Robertson, M 11 B
Poem 1 — Margaret Chambers, C 11 R 1
2 — Gail MacDonald, C 11 R 1
3 — Dolly Kumka, C 11 H 1

To an Artist

Grade 12—Poetry—1st—Gwen McEwen

You walk on surface
smooth as light,
As if some sunless spear
from foreign night,
Will pierce your reverie,
and split the mirror of your birth—
to make you walk a shattered earth.

Tread yet more swiftly,
lost and fearful one,
Lest man in place of shadows
sees you run,
And gives you formless shroud
of laughter—born of tears.
Your sadness now has dampened all my years.

You see an ocean
in a drop of rain,
And fashion, from the master wave
a symphony of pain—
a wistful, soundless note.
This world will not dim your inspiring sun.
All earth shall not tame you—distant one.

Panther Night

—Poetry—1st

Stalking day with eyes of Satan;
Sinews rippling as river flows;
Velvet divinity—paw soft-treading—
What alien dares watch—what hunter knows
Your path?
Enigma in ebony—fathomless
  In sea beyond sun's mirrored wall.
Are you animal or dream remembered—
Beast incarnate? Beauty boundless? All
You are.
Born of wind, sired by eternity,
Pinionless o'er earth's young face;
Without a sound you steal in silence,
Soon to pounce in cold embrace
Of day.
Dawn's silver shaft pierces—night ebbs
In treacherous splendour—yet untold.
A giant cat, in agony, slinks
Towards oblivion—its great form bold
In death.

GWEN MCEWEN

1. If you leave school – then what's the next move?

2. Are Aunty + Uncle aware of your intentions? After all, they have stated, that in spite of anything which happens, they will see you through U of T.
→ Remind me to mention this again

3. Suppose you miss Matriculation. Is this going to debar you from entering your chosen career? Its difficult to find a job of any kind without this qualification

4/. If your driving desire is to write, the only answer is TO WRITE, WRITE, WRITE. Are you going to starve in the meantime?

5/ What do you hope to BE?

Westward Ho!

The Praying Mantis

Grade 12—Story—1st—Gwen McEwen, M12G

"Hypocrite!" He flung the word at her - searing, red-hot syllables that burned a path through the worlds between them.

"Who are you, Valerie, to stand there with that black halo over your head?" How do you dare to enter a holy place, and pretend, for one hour every Sunday that you are a believer? You come back and live the rest of the week in your ungodly feminine world of vicious pursuits and material idolatry. Do you think that when you enter the doors of a church you automatically shed the shell of the liar you are?" He turned away in disgust.

She looked at her husband, and cursed herself for the thousandth time for marrying him.

"You're a fool, Eric," she said slowly. "You spend your time buried in those stupid books of yours. You've read of every religion in existence - studied them, criticized them, and where has it gotten you? You can't call yourself a Christian, a Jew, or anything else. At least I am something. By the way, dear, I do wish you would put in an appearance with me at Church. The girls are starting to talk. Last Sunday no one at all noticed my new dress, because they were too busy asking me where you were. Why I really - - - - "

He turned and faced her then. His eyes were like molten bronze, piercing through her.

"At least I do not lie, Valerie. I believe in God in my own way, and I don't pretend to follow a given religion which is opposed to my greatest beliefs." His voice was deathly quiet, and he uttered a short laugh, pointing to a large praying mantis that was crawling through the door from outside.

"There is your brother, Valerie. It lives in a position of prayer, but cannot even conceive of God. Look at it - see yourself. Mohammed said, 'A painful doom awaits them that lie.' "

She was facing the other way then, and did not see him creep up behind her. She did not see the glint of the knife, either, until it was to late.

He looked at the lifeless body of his wife on the floor. The hideous insect was crawling toward it. In an inaudible, whispering voice, Eric hissed, "Hypocrites - both of you," and crushed the mantis under his heel.

Westward Ho!

The Human Animal

Grade 12—Article—1st—Gwen McEwan M 12 G

Man, the master, having been given a mind—the link between body and spirit, intended to raise him above the prison of mere materialism—holds, now as always, dominion over the earth. The great irony throughout life as some see it is that man has not utilized this mental gift to its fullest extent. In fact, he has not used it in its proper setting. Here, on a mountain of wrought iron and steel, he surveys his domain, and says triumphantly,

"I have conquered the land, been victorious over a giant called the sea, surpassed the swiftest bird, and split the heavens with a sound of thunder."

All this is, of course, beyond denial. He has made the living earth a silent, but undefeated slave to his power, but where and when did he leave his greater, God-given power, behind? At what point did he close the door on the golden realms of the spirit, and venture into the stifling tunnel of the material world? In what lost river did he pour out the wine of senses, worlds upon worlds yet unexplored by the limitless armies of the mind?

We are not here, on this hard pile of rocks and mountains, only to stumble and grope our way through life, always seeking fulfillment for the body, and the more shallow recesses of our untrained minds. If this were so, we would not be man—we would not hold supremacy over the animal kingdom, because we ourselves would be nothing more than exceptionally intellegent animals.

Man refuses to conceive of a greater destiny than the perfection of the material world, and of mental capacities. He will not reach out and clasp the immaterial world of his own higher senses, because he does not believe in its existance.

So we now stand within an empire that has forgotten its own enchanted beauty, and given itself in fierce surrender to a dim and fruitless pursuit. The empire is man, who, by advancing to tremendous heights in the unrewarding world of matter, has succeeded only in lowering himself to the status of something just above mere animalism.

Spiritual perfection, the unspoken birthright of humanity, will never be achieved, because man will not see the need for its achievement. If he did, he would turn around and start walking another path.

Dear Dad,

I seem to have a devil of a problamn all of a sudden, and I thougjt if wrote and told you all about it, then by the time I see you this Sunday, we could talk it over.

This is the first time in my life that I have ever even remotely thought of and this fact alone makes it even more frightening to me, and yet, I am beginning to realize that it has more or less been sleeping within me for quite a while now, and has just recently come to the surface.

The fact is I have lost all interest in school entirely. Now I'll try and explain it to you thoroughly so you won't think I have been brain - washed or something. I realize that a lot of people start getting very restless at my age - it's just natural. But I don't want you to think that this is the only reason for my feelings - - it is perhaps the very smallest reason actually. Just in the last year or so I have become suddenly and acutely aware of what is going on around me - more so than ever before. Now I know that this fact alone is nothing, but the point is that there is something in me which is struggling to come to the surface, but it is cramped and hemmed in simply because I must devote my energy into channels which seem to completely contradict my beliefs and convictions. In other words, I want to be able to put all my thoughts and energy into one direction alone - - and as things stand now, I am unable to do this. Completely unable. I find myself getting more and more frustrated and irritable, because I see so much that I can achieve - I MUST ACHIEVE, and yet I am forced to over look this and devote my time to studies which have become nothing more than worthless.

I must write. I must express myself, or I can't stand it. In school I spend most of my time scribbling bits of poetry, and thinking of the world outside, and the people - - people whom you know, are my greatest love.

Gwendolyn

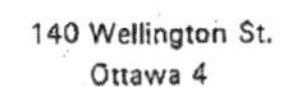

THE CANADA COUNCIL

April 16, 1970.

Miss Gwendolyn MacEwen,
11 Locust Street,
Toronto 335, Ontario.

Dear Miss McEwen:

Further to our letter of February 20th, it gives me great pleasure to advise you that you are among the recipients of the Governor General's Literary Awards for 1969 for your book The Shadow-Maker.

Gwendolyn MacEwen
Gwendolyn MacEwen was born in Toronto in 1941 and died there in 1987. Her first poem was published in the *Canadian Forum* at age 17. Through her impressive bibliography encompassing short fiction, novels, children's books, a travel book and nearly a dozen books of poetry, she displayed a poetic sensibility infused with intelligence, passion and imagination. In 1969 she won the Governor General's Award for English-language poetry for *The Shadow-Maker.* When she died last year at age 46, she had just published her 11th collection of poetry and her first in five years, *Afterworlds.*

Governor-General's Award for poetry goes to MacEwen

BY STEPHEN GODFREY
The Globe and Mail

CALGARY

THE LATE Gwendolyn MacEwen has won the 1987 Governor-General's Award for poetry, it was announced yesterday in Calgary, the first time the presentations have been held in that city.

The award went to MacEwen for Afterworlds (McClelland and Stewart). She won in the same category in 1969.

Poet Gwendolyn MacEwen dead

By Ken Adachi Toronto Star

Gwendolyn MacEwen, the novelist, playwright and poet who won the Governor-General's award in 1969 for her poetry collection, *The Shadow-Maker*, died suddenly yesterday afternoon in her Toronto home. She was 46. Cause of death was not immediately known.

She was a dedicated writer and a major presence in Canadian literature. Born in Toronto, she published her first poem in *The Canadian Forum* and left Western Technical School in 1959 in the middle of grade 13 to pursue a literary career.

"Attending university," she once told me, "wasn't going to make a writer out of me. So many people become inhibited by the writers they study and then can't find their own voice."

Her literary output included two novels, *Julian The Magician* and *King Of Egypt, King Of Dreams*; a short-story collection, *Noman*; two children's books, *The Chocolate Moose* and *The Honey Drum*; and *Mermaids And Ikons*, a travel book based on her visits to Greece.

Gwendolyn MacEwen: Novelist, playwright and poet died yesterday at age 46.

The titles are suggestive of her preoccupation with myth, dream and magic as inextricable links with the big and small events of every day life. Her main preoccupation, however, was poetry.

"I am dedicated to the process, the joy of poetry," she once said in an early interview. The dedication was unswerving, even if her personal life was occasionally difficult. In a poem, part of a collection, *Afterwords*, which was published this spring by McClelland & Stewart, she wrote: "All I have ever cared about/ And all you should ever care about/ Is what happens when you lift your eyes from this page."

She published about a dozen volumes of poetry, each one seeming to be technically more advanced and yet remaining striking in their universal themes of love, loss, anguish and hope. The real tyranny for her, she said, was the alienated self, "the bleak, lunar landscapes of our mirrors. Poetry can help lift readers out of the specifics of pain and suffering, allow them to go back into themselves and then look at the stars."

At the same time, she had an extraordinary, often surreal and powerful imagination. Linked with her verbal and rhythmic flair, it perhaps reached its apotheosis in *The T.E. Lawrence Poems* (1982). She could be fey and cheeky, too. Among her familiar poems, she wrote of a dinner at the old Savarin tavern becoming a feast for cannibals; of a fire in the hearth recreating the city outside as a primeval winter waste; of jewelry as "a glittering prison" taming the wearer.

She was married briefly to poet Milton Acorn around the time she published her first poetry chapbook in 1961. Her second marriage in 1971 to the Greek singer Nikos Tsingos lasted six years, during which time they operated a coffee house called The Trojan Horse on Danforth Ave. and played the music of Mikis Theodorakis and other composers whose works were then banned in Greece.

Details of arrangements for a funeral or memorial service were not known.

Poet won Governor-General's Award

The Globe and Mail

Gwendolyn MacEwen, a Canadian poet who won the Governor-General's Award for English-language poetry, died on Sunday in her Toronto home of undetermined causes. She was 46.

Her body was discovered by a visitor on Monday.

First published in 1961, Ms MacEwen was the author of more than 20 books of poetry, fiction, theatre and travel writing. She was known primarily for her poetry.

Her best-known works included The Armies of the Moon, Magic Animals and Earthlight. More recently, she published Afterworlds, and Dragon Sandwiches, a poetry book for children.

In 1986, Ms MacEwen was writer-in-residence at the University of Toronto. But, like many writers, she found it difficult to make a living from her work.

In a letter that appeared in The Globe and Mail last year, she wrote with tongue in cheek that writers were "a money-grubbing lot."

"I still find myself acting in selfish and irritating ways . . . contacting publishers who have owed me money. . . . Is this not greedy and improper to the extreme? Especially since those sums of money would go to such trifles as rent, food and so on."

Ms MacEwen was married briefly to another Canadian poet, Milton Acorn. Her second marriage in 1971 was to the Greek singer Nikos Tsingos. The marriage lasted six years.

Memorial service planned for poet

The Globe and Mail

A memorial service for the late poet Gwendolyn MacEwen will be held at 8 p.m. Jan. 20 at the Jane Mallett Theatre of the St. Lawrence Centre in Toronto.

MacEwen died in November at the age of 46.

Literary broadcaster Robert Weaver will be the host at the service, being organized by writers Michael Ondaatje and David Donnell with the co-operation of MacEwen's sister, Carol Wilson.

Weaver will speak briefly, as will Wilson. About 10 writers, including Al Purdy, Timothy Findley, Joe Rosenblatt, Margaret Atwood and Phyllis Webb, will read from MacEwen's work.

Admission is free.

Related Reading

Poetry

Selah, Aleph Press, Toronto, 1961.

The Drunken Clock, Aleph Press, Toronto, 1961.

The Rising Fire, Contact Press, Toronto, 1963.

A Breakfast for Barbarians, The Ryerson Press, Toronto, 1966.

The Shadow-Maker, Macmillan, Toronto, 1969.

The Armies of the Moon, Macmillan, Toronto, 1972.

Magic Animals: Selected Poems Old and New, Macmillan, Toronto, 1974.

The Fire Eaters, Oberon Press, Ottawa, 1976.

Trojan Women: The Trojan Women by Euripedes and *Helen* and *Orestes* by Yannis Ritsos; translated with Nikos Tsingos, Exile Editions, Toronto, 1981.

The T.E. Lawrence Poems, Mosaic Press, Oakville, 1982.

Earth-Light: Selected Poetry 1963–1982, General Publishing, Toronto, 1982.

Afterworlds, McClelland and Stewart, Toronto, 1987.

The Poetry of Gwendolyn MacEwen: The Early Years (Volume One), eds. Margaret Atwood and Barry Callaghan, Exile Editions, 1993.

The Poetry of Gwendolyn MacEwen: The Later Years (Volume Two), eds. Margaret Atwood and Barry Callaghan, Exile Editions, 1994.

Novels

Julian the Magician, Corinth Books, New York; Macmillan, Toronto, 1963.

King of Egypt, King of Dreams, Macmillan, Toronto, 1971.

Short Stories

Noman, Oberon Press, Ottawa, 1972.

Noman's Land, The Coach House Press, Toronto, 1985.

Travel

Mermaids and Ikons: A Greek Summer, House of Anansi, Toronto, 1978.

Theatre

The Trojan Women, Playwrights Co-op, Toronto, 1979.

The Birds, A Modern Adaptation, Exile Editions, 1993.

Biography

Shadow Maker: The Life of Gwendolyn MacEwen, by Rosemary Sullivan, Harper Collins, Toronto, 1995.

Questions for Discussion and Essays

1. One of Gwendolyn MacEwen's primary interests lay in the structuring of a mythic reality wherein she sets in opposition the works of children, magicians, escape artists, adventurers, the barbaric and the divinely mad to grown-ups, bureaucrats, the solid and the stolid, the tamed among the tamers. Provide examples of how she does this, and explain her use of juxtaposition.

2. As Margaret Atwood has pointed out, one of the paradoxes of Gwendolyn MacEwen's work is that the protagonists she chooses – the personae – are almost invariably male. MacEwen speaks in a female voice when addressing a male lyrically "I" to "You" – but when she uses a dramatic form or writes a poem about a heroic figure, the central character is usually a man. Discuss the implications as you see them of this paradox

3. In the poem "Certain Flowers" do the flowers have negative or positive attributes?

4. "The Dimensions of a Tiger" – Does the title of this poem refer to only the physical dimensions of a tiger, or what other dimensions does it examine?

5. What are the topics touched on in the poem "A Breakfast for Barbarians"? What is the conceit of this poem?

6. "Poem Improvised Around a First Line" – What do you think the first line of this poem would have been?

7. “Manzini: Escape Artist” – What does the escape artist represent in this poem?

8. In *The Lonliest Country In the World* why does MacEwen use Kanada instead of Canada?

9. “Dark Pines Under Water” – What role does alliteration play in this poem?

10. “Hypnos” – Why is this poem entitled “Hynos?”

11. In her later poems, Gwendolyn MacEwen reveals a preoccupation wirh time and its multiple meanings; with the ambivalences of existence; and with the archetypal patterns that emerge and re-emerge from ancient times to now. Discuss the uses, the roles, to which she puts time and archetypal patterns in her poetry.

12. Gwendolyn MacEwen’s final poems are marked by an affirmation of life she found in physics, expressed particularly in her poem, “The Tao of Physics” in which she directly challenges Death. Discuss.

13. In Gwendolyn MacEwen’s fiction, she gives us her imaginative re-construction of historical figures and her construction of fantasy figures who are equally engaged in the gallant but futile attempt to transcend death, to rise like a bird out of the ashes, like the light nourished by darkness. Is this the age-old attempt to redeem life through the word, through language?

14. Who does Julian think is his contemporary? What qualities support and which qualities oppose this conclusion?

15. What are Julian's mixed emotions about his audience?

16. Describe one of Julian's tricks, and how this trick reveals insights into his personality.

17. For a poet/writer such as MacEwen, how do faith and art relate to each other?

Related URLs

www.library.utoronto.ca/canpoetry/macewen/index.htm
—biography, poems, writing philosophy, published works

en.wikipedia.org/wiki/Gwendolyn_MacEwen
—bibliography, discography, external links

www.youngpoets.ca/rebels/macewen.php
—portrait poet, interesting facts

www.gwenpark.org
—Memorial Park

www.brocku.ca/canadianwomenpoets/Macewen.htm
—works, criticism, award, biography

thecanadianencyclopedia.com/index.cfm?PgNm=TCE&Para
ms=A1ARTA0004893
—biography

www.chbooks.com/archives/online_books/nomans_land
—online excerpts from *Noman's Land*

www.rosemarysullivan.com/books.html
—*Shadow Maker: The Life of Gwendolyn MacEwen*,
by Rosemary Sullivan

www.luxphoto.com
—The artwork of Tony Clark